Best wishes
Joe Fowler

Harvest of Riches

Harvest of Riches

A Guide for Young
Entrepreneurs and Families

Joe R. Fowler, PhD
with Pamela Fannin Wilkinson

Copyright © 2019 by Joe R. Fowler, PhD.

Library of Congress Control Number:		2019902735
ISBN:	Hardcover	978-1-7960-2028-1
	Softcover	978-1-7960-2027-4
	eBook	978-1-7960-2026-7

All rights reserved. No part of this book may be reproduced or transmitted in any form or by any means, electronic or mechanical, including photocopying, recording, or by any information storage and retrieval system, without permission in writing from the copyright owner.

Print information available on the last page.

Rev. date: 03/13/2019

To order additional copies of this book, contact:
Xlibris
1-888-795-4274
www.Xlibris.com
Orders@Xlibris.com

Contents

Preface vii
With Gratitude ix

1. Joe's Backstory 1
2. Times Have Changed 8
3. Charting a Course 13
4. The Strawberry Tub 24
5. Crafting Stress Engineering Services Inc. 31
6. Stress Engineering Services Inc. and Industry History 68
7. The Importance of Goal Setting 71
8. Technologies of Tomorrow 74
9. Hindsight's Perspective: Tips for Success and Giving Back 79
10. Granddaddy's Investing Advice 86
11. Granddaddy's Summer Camp 90
12. Grandchildren's Advice for Raising Kids 94

Timeline 99
Resources 103
About the Author 105

PREFACE

I embarked on this project to try to pass on to the next generation what Linda and I have learned about business and families. I am fortunate to have an experienced writer, Pam Wilkinson, as my coauthor. Hopefully, together we can give you, the reader, information that will be useful to you.

If you have a desire to start a business (any business), I think the principles in this book will help you. It tells the stories of widely divergent businesses and how their success comes back to passion, hard work, and good values. It goes through the checklist of principles and what to do and consider in charting a course. The detailed stories of the retailers, the Strawberry Tub (Linda's business) and Stress Engineering Services (the engineering and testing company I cofounded), show the application of the principles. Both applied the principles of doing what we loved, working hard, and giving back.

As an engineer who grew up with the technologies of yesterday and today, I will give you my opinion of the technologies of tomorrow. Perhaps that will help you in the search for your passion and your business.

Finally, Linda and I have been blessed with wonderful, loving children with their spouses, along with nine grandchildren. One of the most important chapters of this book is these grandchildren's advice for raising kids. These grandchildren are ages twelve to twenty-one, five boys and four girls, and I think you will enjoy comparing your wisdom to theirs.

Thank you very much for reading this, and we pray this knowledge will provide blessings to you and your family.

JRF
Houston, Texas

WITH GRATITUDE

First, I want to thank my wife of fifty-three years, Linda McDonald Fowler. She has been my partner, helper, consultant, and friend throughout the whole process of pursuing higher education, raising a family, and building Stress Engineering Services Inc. (SES). The Strawberry Tub was her vision and drive from the beginning. Everything in the book is really a joint project between us, and none of it could or would have happened without her. Her values and sense of right and wrong have always kept me grounded.

Next, I want to thank my partners at SES. Tom Asbill, Dr. Ron Young Dr. Ed Bailey, Jack Miller, Randy Long, Chuck Miller, John Chappell, Jim Albert, Allen Fox, Clint Haynes, Terry Lechinger, Teri Shackelford, and Helen Chan were especially important to the founding of Stress; and many others, many mentioned in the book, were important also.

I want to thank the reviewers who offered many constructive comments that greatly improved the book. They are the professor of practice at Texas A&M University, Jim Donnell; professor at Sam Houston State University, Dr. Joe Kavanaugh; partners Dr. Ron Young, Clint Haynes, and Jack Miller; our children, Jodi Malanga, Rob Fowler, and Amy Shawver; my brother Don Fowler; and Linda's sister Donna McDonald Picou.

Dr. John Hoffmann was not only a reviewer but also an important part of the story as a collaborator in the water heater wars and an inspiration through his business and his family. He was the catalyst for Granddaddy's Summer Camp.

I want to thank all the teachers, administrators, former students, and supporters of Texas A&M University, which provided the foundation of my education and the passion for the consulting business. The values of competence, hard work, and caring about others instilled there remain crucial to success for anyone.

I also want to thank my coauthor, Pamela Fannin Wilkinson, for her hard work, extraordinary skill, and patience at keeping me focused to complete this project. Thank you, Pam!

We especially appreciate the courtesies of the staff of the Schulenburg Public Library in Schulenburg, Texas, for allowing us to meet there many times, halfway between our homes in Houston and San Antonio.

•

One

Joe's Backstory

Wichita Falls is cold in the winter, blazing hot in the summer, and situated less than twenty miles from the Red River, the Texas-Oklahoma state line. The wind blows all the time. The population has grown to nearly 105,000 in 2018, but it has grown very little since I grew up there with my older brothers, David and Don, and my older sister, Rosemary. Our father taught us the value of self-discipline and hard work. Our mother taught us love and compassion and the importance of being mindful of words and other people's feelings. As the youngest of four, my siblings taught me to be tough and to stand up for myself.

My dad knew full well how likely boys were to get into trouble in the summer if they weren't busy. Before he went to work in the morning, he gave us jobs to do. As the summer went on, the jobs became harder. He would have us do jobs like levelling the irrigation ditch from the back of the property and spreading the dirt over the entire property. We always stayed busy and mostly out of trouble.

He was a strict disciplinarian and regularly used the "board of education" when we needed it but always at home. When we were all driving in the car (four kids and my parents) and we misbehaved, he would paddle us when we returned home. Once, we had been on a trip to Fort Worth and were driving home and really got rowdy. Out of exasperation, he said, "If I hear another peep out of you, you'll all get a busting when we get home!" We were quiet for a while, and then my brother Don said softly, "Peep." When we got home, none of us ratted Don out, and we all got a busting.

My mother was a very good mother. Also, during the summer, she took us to the library several days a week, and we became voracious readers. Some of the early lessons I remember from her were when she taught us how to have empathy for others. One of her lessons was that when you say something harsh to someone, it's like shooting an arrow. You can take it out, but it will almost always do a lot of damage.

Mother never hesitated to stand up for people either. For example, my brother Don liked to play football. He tried out for the eighth grade team at Zundy Junior High while he was in the seventh grade. He made it to the team and reported for practice the next fall at Zundy.

At the time, Don was very small, maybe only 101 pounds. The new coach told him, "You can't have a uniform. You're too small." Don went home very upset. Mother marched right up to school and gave the coach a lesson in caring about kids. Don got a uniform and went on to have a great high school football career and was the starting guard on the 1961 Wichita Falls High School state championship team.

As a child, I remember playing with our family dog, Patsy, who was a half-chow and half-German shepherd. She was an outside dog, was very sweet, and was a good guard dog; and we really loved her. When she died, we all grieved. We took a wheelbarrow to a nearby road and brought back a large (for us) piece of finished concrete that had been part of a road marker. We chiseled "PATSY—1948–1958" on it and used it as a tombstone when we buried her in the backyard.

Mother and Dad sold that home in 1980 and moved to Georgetown. Right after their move, they got a frantic call from their realtor, who asked, "Did you bury a child in the backyard?" The new owners had found the tombstone and were very upset!

Like a lot of lower-income families then, we raised chickens. We had a chicken house and a portion of the yard fenced off as a chicken coop. We butchered two chickens most Sundays and also got eggs every day. We learned how to wring a chicken's neck and butcher it, and fresh fried chicken was sooo good!

Every little bit helped. The chicken feed came in sacks made of cotton material printed with various patterns. Mother took that material and made shirts for us. Most of the kids at school never realized it. In elementary school, I worked in the cafeteria at lunch to get a reduced lunch price.

In high school, I was a football player and a good student, and I worked in construction. I started as a laborer at age fourteen for a concrete company. By the time I was a senior in high school, I had become a cement finisher. College looked really good!

As a teenager, I always saved the money I made. By the time I was seventeen or so, I had saved quite a bit (for a kid). Dad was a state employee, raising the four of us, and had no ready cash. He really wanted to buy a piece of property in Wise County, Texas, north of Fort Worth. He could borrow from the Veterans Land Board because he was a World War II veteran, but he didn't have the down payment. So I loaned him the money (about $1,000), and he bought the property.

It had many old-growth pecan trees that were good producers, and Dad hired people who harvested them for half of the crop. He also leased out the land for grazing. Then in a stroke of good luck, the property became part of George Mitchell's original gas fields in North Texas (Mitchell was a Houston oilman and developer of the Woodlands, Texas), and Dad earned mineral royalties from it. When Mother and Dad moved from Wichita Falls to Georgetown, they sold the Wise County property, and it became an important part of their retirement. So it turned out to be a great investment, and I have had a lifelong love for our state tree, the pecan.

Wichita Falls is known as a tornado alley, and while I was growing up, tornadoes came twice within a mile from our house—once to the south and again to the north. Then on April 10, 1979, Wichita Falls drew the short straw when three tornados converged and formed an F4 (devastating) tornado that was one and one-half miles wide. It reduced all the buildings to slabs in a two-and-one-half-mile-long swath of destruction. Forty-six people were killed, many of them in their cars, and some had driven under freeway overpasses for safety. They were killed when the tornado sucked their cars up and crushed the occupants from above. The devastation was horrific.

Probably because of this and a desire to live closer to their children and grandchildren, my parents moved to Georgetown on the July Fourth holiday of 1980. Don and I and our families rented a truck and withstood the goodbye present of 114-degree temperature

Joe's Backstory

and a strong south wind to move them. Wichita Falls produced tough people.

Because times were tight, as the youngest, I had to put myself through college. But in those days, a boy could earn $1,000 in construction during the summer, which was then about the cost of a year at Texas A&M University. And, of course, I went to A&M since both of my brothers went there, and my sister married an Aggie.

I enrolled at A&M in the fall of 1964 and studied mechanical engineering. In my freshmen year, I was in the Corps of Cadets and worked as a waiter in Duncan Dining Hall. Texas A&M was hard academically. Fortunately, Wichita Falls High School was a great school; and I had studied physics, chemistry, and calculus there.

Gen. Earl Rudder was a war hero and was well qualified to lead Texas A&M—first as university president and later as president of the Texas A&M University System. He addressed all of us freshman in the now-demolished Guion Hall. "Gentlemen," he said because all of us were members of an all-male student body, "look at the person on your left and at the person on your right. They are not going to be here when you graduate."

You could have heard a pin drop.

"And furthermore," the general said, "if you don't like the way I operate, Highway 6 runs both ways. You can leave the same way you came in."

So students who did not come from strong schools or had not learned how to study in high school generally did not do well at A&M. In my freshman outfit of thirty men, only four of us graduated from Texas A&M in engineering. The rest left school or changed majors. The percentage of students who actually graduate from the engineering school has dramatically improved today, but those were different times, and a lot of people held the attitude that if you could make it through Texas A&M, you would be a very good engineer. It was a trial by fire.

But the most striking thing about Texas A&M in those days was the culture. I always felt that the staff and my fellow students cared about one another. In those days, most young men were like me and did not have a car, and hitchhiking was a common way to travel. If a student ran out of money or needed help, professors and fellow students would help them. Standards were high, and everyone was expected to do their work, but people really cared about one another.

It is amazing to me that that same spirit pervades Texas A&M to this day, and a great culture still thrives there even though enrollment has grown from eight thousand in 1964 to sixty-eight thousand-plus in 2017. That is where I really learned that good spirit begets good spirit and bad spirit begets bad spirit.

A happy day – Joe and Linda's wedding, 1965.

I married Linda, my high school sweetheart, in 1965, between my freshman and sophomore years; and Dad repaid the Wise County loan on our wedding day. The cash helped us get started on our married life; we celebrated our fiftieth anniversary in 2015. We supported ourselves on Linda's job, my part-time jobs, and scholarships. When times got really tough financially, we picked up glass Coke bottles thrown on the side of the road and turned them in for recycling, which brought anywhere from ten to twenty-five cents apiece. A loaf of bread cost twenty-five cents.

After earning my bachelor's degree, I stayed at Texas A&M and got both a master's and a PhD in mechanical engineering. During my PhD program, several professors also had consulting practices. I helped them with that work and grew to understand and enjoy the consulting engineering business.

By the time I completed my PhD and left A&M, a number of things had started to change. For one thing, the school had improved the dropout rate. That was such a waste of time, money, and resources. Today, the College of Engineering won't admit students without the proper prerequisites. Students either get those in high school or community college, and the mind-set is to graduate as many students as possible to become good, productive citizens. Now 86.9 percent of freshmen students (highest in the state) graduate within six years, against a state average of 60.9 percent.

The other thing that made an enormous difference is that General Rudder saw the significance of admitting women and making the school coeducational. It was a fantastic decision, and without it, Texas A&M would have been just a backwater college instead of a world-class institution.

By the time we left College Station, Linda and I had two precious children. Jodi was born in 1968 and Rob in 1970. Our third child, Amy, was born in 1974 in Houston. All of them were blessed with good health. All of them were raised as Christians, all of them graduated from Texas A&M, and all met their spouses as fellow students while they were in school there.

While a student myself, I was the recipient of generous scholarships from Louis A. Priester of A&M class of 1917—founder of Priester Supply Company in Dallas. These were very important to our family, and we have provided many scholarships at A&M and at an inner-city Houston church (currently more than twenty) to pay it forward. With the increased cost of college, it is vitally important that those who have received this type of help and can provide it to the next generation should pay it forward.

As I mentioned after completing my degrees, we moved to Houston; and I started to work for Texaco in their research and development department. I was with them for two years and fortunately spent most of my time doing measurement projects on the drilling rigs. In those days, Texaco owned three or four drilling rigs, and I had a lot of freedom on them. It was a great hands-on experience for a young engineer because I quickly came to understand the equipment, how it operated, and the challenges of a field operation, where safety is crucial to success.

After two years with Texaco, one of my former professors and an older friend asked me to join them in establishing a consulting firm, which I did in 1972. We founded the firm that is today Stress Engineering Services Inc. (Stress), now with almost four hundred employees and offices in Houston, Waller, New Orleans, Baton Rouge, Cincinnati, Calgary, and Singapore. In addition to building an engineering consulting and test lab business, Linda and I also ran a successful retail chain of Hallmark cards and gift stores in the earlier days.

I became president of Stress Engineering Services Inc. in 1984 and remained in that position until I semiretired in 2015 and sold most of my shares in the company back to SES. During the thirty-one years I was president and we were building the firm, I learned a tremendous amount about customers, partners, employees, ethics, and the management of businesses.

•

Two

Times Have Changed

The world I entered when I came to Texas A&M was far different from that of today. In the 1960s, an engineer would typically keep three or four draftsmen busy. He designed, and they drew. Today, draftsmen are disappearing, replaced by a far fewer number of computer-aided design (CAD) operators, and much-routine design of similar products is actually done by a computer program written by an engineer or by a programmer under the direction of an engineer.

Product development was long. The costly steps of design, prototype construction, test, redesign, reprototype, and so on could take years. Engineering, marketing, and manufacturing often did not communicate well. Today, product development time has been dramatically shortened through the use of CAD, better internal communications, and advanced manufacturing techniques. Finite element analysis, which is a particular specialty of our company, Stress Engineering Services Inc., has progressed to the point that most of the cuts and tries are done on the computer screen rather than on the laboratory floor.

United States's foreign trade was relatively small in the 1960s. Imports and exports were about 4 percent of GDP in 1968. Today, they are about 30 percent. More than 50 percent of the energy we used was imported. Companies were developing more contacts internationally.

By 1991, while the larger American companies dealt with every major nation, Stress had business dealings with organizations in

Japan, Germany, Canada, Mexico, Argentina, People's Republic of China, Taiwan, Saudi Arabia, England, Ireland, and Norway. Today, that includes Brazil, Trinidad, Argentina, United Arab Emirates, and Colombia; and Stress has offices in Canada and Singapore.

In the 1960s, many products and procedures were shoddy. Remember the Ford Pinto, which had a nasty habit of catching on fire when hit from behind, or the Chevrolet Corvair? Ralph Nader wrote *Unsafe at Any Speed* about the Corvair. Remember the spinning chain on a drill pipe? Many, many fingers were lost because of that inherently unsafe procedure. Although cars have been greatly improved and the spinning chain has become a relic from the past, many areas still need quality improvement today.

In thermodynamics, we did our problems then on a slide rule. After leaving Dr. Simmang's thermo class, we joked that our sticks had to be cooled under the water fountain. Today, engineers have programmable calculators and computers that greatly increase the speed of the work and dramatically enhance the presentation quality.

In 1970, the computer on campus at Texas A&M was an IBM 7094 that had punch card input, required a computer science major to set up the job control language (JCL), and was speed wise, about on a par with an IBM 8086 PC of the early 1980s. Plotting was a major problem and was usually done by hand with a Leroy inking set. Today, every engineer at our company has an advanced PC, and the cell phone he or she carries is at least one thousand times faster than the 1970 computers and stores one hundred times the data. The advent of spreadsheet programs also has dramatically increased the depth and quality of our engineering calculation work. However, the best professors always have concentrated on teaching fundamental principles and teaching students the process of design. This is one area where nothing has changed.

Many major industries of the day were very cyclical, and they still are. When I earned my BS in 1968, the petroleum and aerospace industries were doing well, and I had ten job offers. By the time I earned the PhD in 1971, both industries were in a recession, and not one single company came to A&M to recruit PhD engineers. I thought maybe I had made a mistake! It turned out to be a good thing for personal development since I had to learn to hustle and sell myself to employers. I wrote lots of letters and made lots of phone calls, and before I graduated, I had three job offers. I took one of them, and fellow graduate students took the other two.

The aerospace industry was in a down position throughout most of the 1970s until Ronald Reagan started his military buildup in the early 1980s. Today, with greatly increased air travel and booming private space programs, the industry is robust. The petroleum industry has fared worse as far as stability is concerned. The president of McDermott Industries said that their economic research shows that since the year 1900, the petroleum industry has undergone a series of business cycles, each approximately twenty years long. In my career, the worst ones were the mid-1980s and between 2015 and 2017.

The petroleum industry was predicted to be up during most of the 1990s, but the mid-1980s had been a devastating time for petroleum. Sales at the largest—and one of the strongest—oil field service firms, Halliburton, declined by 60 percent between 1981 and 1987. Sales at Varco, typical of the smaller firms in the same period, declined by 80 percent! Employment followed suit. Similar declines happened in 2016–2017.

We have been in a bust for the offshore industry since about 2015, but the land-based petroleum industry now is recovering from low prices with the development of horizontal drilling, pioneered by the same George Mitchell, who paid my dad gas royalties. The automotive industry also has had a series of wrenching ups and downs throughout its history. Solar and wind energy presently promise to make large inroads into the conventional fossil fuel industry, and autonomous electric cars are on the horizon.

In spite of the cyclical nature of industry, many companies offered essentially lifetime employment to their professional staff; and in return, the companies expected lifetime loyalty. Unfortunately, this is very rare today. Most companies do not hesitate to downsize when current economic conditions call for it. As a small company, Stress, fortunately, has not had to do this to any great extent, but almost all large companies have.

Back in the day, internal communications in many companies were horrible. During my first job in the research department of a major oil company, my colleague and I could not communicate directly with our counterparts in the operating divisions. Communications had to be up two levels, over, and down two levels. Needless to say, there was little information exchange. In many manufacturing companies, engineering, sales, and production rarely communicated except for formal documents.

Purchasers of industrial equipment were not sophisticated, and sales claims were often exaggerated. Today, major companies have become very sophisticated purchasers and may delve deeply into the design, manufacturing, and testing of products they buy. This is frequently done through hired third-party engineers and testing organizations such as Stress.

One of the reasons for this rigorous testing is that failures have become so expensive. The legal industry has become very large. In 2006, there were about 1.5 million engineers and 760,000 lawyers in the US. A hungry plaintiff attorney is waiting to capitalize on every failure. For a number of years, the major thrust of the American Petroleum Institute, which is a standard writing organization for the petroleum industry, has been *quality*. The twin threats of foreign competition, particularly Japanese and Chinese, and fear of large judgments have done wonders for our basic manufacturing quality.

In the 1960s, the fumes from leaded gasoline in almost any large city were stifling. Today, because of the federal ban on leaded gasoline, that situation has improved immensely. Today, leaded gasoline has mostly been phased out worldwide.

In some areas, however, we've gotten worse. Houston home movies taken in 1958 of Galveston Bay and from the top of the San Jacinto Monument show clean blue water and few chemical plants. These industrial plants have brought great prosperity, but the environmental price paid was understood in the 1980s and '90s each time you drove in Pasadena, Texas City, or Beaumont and smelled the air. This has improved dramatically in the last fifteen to twenty years and will no doubt improve in the future—primarily from regulation due to the Clean Air Act of 1970, the EPA (established in 1970), and state and local laws. The EPA was established after the Santa Barbara oil spill of 1969. Incidentally, this spill led to the US Coast Guard funding the development of a new floating oil containment barrier, which was the subject of my PhD dissertation at Texas A&M.

In short, this brief history teaches us that technology has dramatically advanced in all fields and will continue to do so. The

Times Have Changed

constant change of industries and business practices will continue unabated. Everyone, particularly technical people, will have to work to remain relevant to changing industries. And finally, all this is challenging but exciting.

●

Three

Charting a Course

When starting a business, a person needs to address certain questions pretty much in a prescribed fashion. Thinking them through is helpful, time-saving, and affirmative in establishing what you want to do and how to go about it.

First, ask yourself, What business am I in, or what business do I want to be in?

For me, it was easy. I had seen successful professionals operating consulting engineering businesses. I had worked in those businesses myself and liked the work. It utilized the technical skills in which I had been trained. In fact, the main reason for pursuing a PhD was to enable me to be successful in the consulting engineering business. I also had seen that the financial rewards of the consulting business could be very good. For my wife, Linda, it was also easy in deciding to establish the card and gift stores. She loved the creative side of retail and loved shopping and became a Texas master florist.

But for you, what business should it be? I think there are two main factors to consider. The most important question is, What is your passion? Starting a business is an extremely difficult task, and most businesses do not succeed. To be successful, you have to be doing something you love. This is also the way to be the best at that business. It's not work if you love it! The second factor to consider is that the business needs to be in an industry and market area where you can achieve significant financial success. If you're going to work yourself very hard for a number of years and risk all your money and more, you need a reward to stay motivated. Your decision also should allow you to have the means and money to keep employees and partners happy.

By the same token, if you love the business but can't make any money at it, then it's a hobby, not a business. If you can make money but hate the work, what kind of a life is that? Your business should have both virtues. To find it, you may need to look in a lot of places and try a number of things. One of the best aspects of pursuing education in college or elsewhere is the number of opportunities to explore.

At Stress Engineering Services Inc., our business has always been about helping customers solve their hardest technical challenges. This started in the nuclear industry, switched to the offshore oil industry, added the pipeline and refinery industries in the mid-'80s, added the consumer products industry in the early '90s, and added materials engineering in the mid-'90s. Today, a new focus is handling and making sense out of big data, like that collected when monitoring equipment such as pipelines, refineries, offshore platforms, and manufacturing facilities.

At Stress, we were asked many times over the years to develop products for a piece of the action. A client would offer us stock in their company or a percentage of the sales of the product in return for designing it for them. Sometimes an employee or partner would have the idea to do this. As a matter of policy, we decided not to do that.

One of the big attractions to clients is that Stress did not have a dog in the hunt and offered only impartial advice. If we had developed our own design for any product, we would automatically be disqualified from participating in projects where we were evaluating or testing our products or any competitor's product. Over the years, we were served well by that policy. Clients trusted us since we did not have ulterior motives.

The only patents we kept were those having to do with the equipment in our labs or equipment we used to perform services at clients' facilities. We developed a lot of equipment for clients, and many of our people were the authors of many patents (Jack Miller has more than forty), but Stress was not the owner of these patents. Thinking through what business we were in and what business we were not in was central to the success of Stress.

In the 1980s, Stress's business suffered like the entire oil industry from a depression in the industry. We were looking for business in other areas, and fortunately, one of our software suppliers knew of our high-quality work and also knew that Procter & Gamble (P&G) was looking for a firm to solve hard technical problems for them. So the software firm made an introduction, and we began doing some projects for P&G.

One of our first projects was solving a problem about shampoo bottles. The shampoo bottle leaked, and when the shampoo leaked on the customer's groceries on the way home from the store, it was a consumer negative that really hurt P&G sales. In fact, it was reported to us that P&G had lost many hundreds of millions of dollars on these kinds of failures. So Stress applied the sealing technology that we had developed on oil patch products, and with the aid of advanced software, we were able to solve their issues. Procter & Gamble became an important customer for many years.

Then in the early 2000s, P&G asked us to open an office in Cincinnati, and that was the basis for our Cincinnati consumer products business that continues to this day. Thanks to Allen Fox, who actually solved the shampoo bottle problem and for being the customer contact person. Clint Haynes was our first P&G customer representative and now is the vice president of Stress over all our consumer products business. At our fortieth anniversary celebration in 2012, our Cincinnati office reported that *they had saved over one billion pounds of plastic* for our clients.

The second thing to ask is, How do I find customers?

Many people who want to be business owners and entrepreneurs have great difficulty talking to potential customers and, more importantly, listening to what they say. Talking and writing to convince and to educate are key technical skills, but the most important skill is listening.

Many entrepreneurs have great ideas for a service or product but don't understand why the customers don't buy it. There is a reason, if the entrepreneur will listen closely enough. So finding customers has to be one of the first things that you do in a business or in a business that you would like to pursue. They can be found in many places, depending on the type of business.

Charting a Course

You have to find your customers, you have to be able to listen to them, and you have to continue to find them and listen to them even as your business grows. In fact, the larger a business grows, the more important it is that this skill of finding and listening becomes one of the key strategies of the company. Conferences, sales calls, working in volunteer organizations, and internet survey skills are all part of this. Big consumer products companies continuously use focus groups of real consumers to understand their customers.

Mistakes here are very costly or even fatal. For example, in the 1990s, a client came to us needing help with the severe failures they had experienced in the piping and fittings they used to perform high-pressure pumping at their customers' sites all over the United States. Their US headquarters' safety department wanted Stress to set up a roving test service that would go to each of their yards, or local base of operations, on a regular basis and pressure test and inspect their "iron," as this piping was called.

So we did a business plan and hired and trained new technicians and procured the necessary test equipment and started this service at their fifteen or so nationwide locations. At first, things went great and seemed a good fit both for us and for them. But over time, we found that not all the locations actually used Stress. Some started using low-cost and low-quality companies that were the favorite of the local manager. That is when we discovered that the headquarters' safety department did not have the authority to direct or use our services as they had represented to us since the local operations had profit or loss responsibility for their local operations.

This was a mistake on our part and could have been a very costly error. We shut down the service. Fortunately, our lab business had grown to the point where all the employees doing this service were transferred to our laboratories, and they turned out to be great new employees.

Third, ask yourself, where do I get the money to start a business?
Financing obviously depends on the type of business you are starting. If you're going to develop a product to manufacture and sell, then the money required naturally depends on the cost to develop the product, the cost to manufacture it, and the cost to sell it. If you are going into the services business, then you often can start on a small scale with a smaller investment and build the business over time

as you add clients and people to perform the services. If you're going into the retail business, you obviously have to fund the inventory in the store, the start-up expenses of the store, the training of the people, and the cash flow until the business sustains itself.

This is the reason why you really need to do a business plan, which is simply a plan for the business with dollar signs and schedules and budgets. Depending on the amount of capital you need, this plan will determine where you might get it. If the amount is modest, then perhaps you can get it from your savings or your family. If the amount is more substantial, then you will have to go to a venture capitalist or an angel investor to get money to start.

Many entrepreneurs automatically think of banks for financing. Among the things banks want is a collateral or assets they can seize to repay the loan if you can't. Banks will tell you that their profit is just getting the interest on the money they loan so they don't want to take any chance that they won't actually get their money back. And if your collateral is not good enough for them, they will ask you to personally guarantee the loan. This means if you can't repay the loan, they can seize your personal property (like your house) to repay it.

Therefore, you must always respect and keep your banker well informed about the business, with never any unpleasant surprises. Eventually, when there is no real risk of nonpayment, the banks will forgo personal guarantees. Then after you have a track record of business with the risk mostly out of it, you can qualify for bank financing. Another avenue is the Small Business Administration, which has a program that can relax borrowing requirements for some start-ups.

Along these lines, it is also very important that you pay your federal income taxes, and especially the taxes withheld from your employees to pay their taxes, your employer taxes, and your state and local taxes. The IRS has tremendous power and can seize all your money and property if you don't pay them. Please don't ignore them!

We purchased our main building at 13800 Westfair East in Houston from the bank after it foreclosed on the structure, which had been built for a company that manufactured hyperbaric chambers for hospitals. These chambers could be pressurized with pure oxygen to three atmospheres, which was very good for treating burn patients. The manufacturing company sold several of them to hospitals in

Saudi Arabia. They shipped the chambers to Saudi Arabia but never got paid. Their only recourse was bankruptcy.

Fortunately for us, the bank wanted to get this building off their books and sold it to us for half of what it had cost to build less than two years earlier. And because Stress had good credit, they financed it for us at a very attractive rate. From this, we learned that we never extended credit to a customer where default could really hurt us, and foreign sales were done with letters of credit with the money deposited before we shipped.

As another example of financial reckoning, when our company was first formed with me, Harry Sweet, and Ray Latham, we had a line of credit to advance money for receivables. After a year or so, Ray left our company to start a manufacturing firm, which was really his passion. He had set up the line of credit, so Harry and I went to talk to the bank.

The banker told us, "Well, your line of credit was based on Ray's finances, so we will have to start over with you." Fortunately, it all worked out, but there were some sleepless nights. From this, I learned to always have a backup bank.

Stress was funded with capital from shareholders, retained earnings, and bank financing. Your planning skills will serve you well here. Just remember one of the fundamental laws of business, and that is about cash. Cash is like the blood of a business. When you run out of cash, you die no matter how strong the rest of the business is. Remember, if you ever miss a payroll, even once, employees may leave and will certainly lose confidence in you.

Fourth, ask yourself, Do I need partners?

This is a fundamental question for anyone going into business, and the answer depends on you and the business. As the ancient Greeks said, "Know thyself."

Many people have a dream of becoming one of the wealthiest in the country. The Koch brothers, the Mars family, and the S. C. Johnson family, among others, own huge businesses that do not have to answer to the demands of the public market and have tremendous wealth and freedom. Many of the largest donors to colleges and universities are the owners of companies that have grown very large and profitable. If that is your passion, you should be very careful about taking on partners. If the business is successful, you will have to become adept at motivating and rewarding partners in order for it to continue to grow and be successful.

Fifth, ask yourself, Do I have a need to be in charge, or can I share authority?

The unfolding answer to this question also depends on the business itself. A professional practice of any type—lawyer, doctor, engineer, accountant, or even hair care professional—is more naturally stable when the business is owned by the professionals. It is natural for customers to feel more loyal to the service provider than to the firm itself, and many customers will follow the professional rather than the firm.

If the professionals have established a good, collegial, and fair structure, then the practice can be very stable, providing the freedom to share work for everyone's benefit. Of course, it usually takes a considerable period for any professional to develop to the point of handling clients, so good partnerships have training and mentoring programs to encourage this.

The answer also depends on the capital requirements of the business. If it is a firm to develop a new product, capital requirements are likely to be significant. If it is a business to buy or develop real estate, the capital requirements likewise will probably be significant. If it is a business to do consulting or other personal service, the capital requirements will likely be more modest.

Whatever the business is and whatever the capital requirements are, it is a fundamental responsibility of you, the entrepreneur, to raise that money. Do I need partners to do that? Do I need partners to conduct the business? Are there tasks involved in the business that I can't do and that I need help to accomplish? There is always the possibility of simply hiring an employee to do tasks that you are not qualified to do yourself. But to inject capital into the business, most folks will expect an equity partnership.

My son-in-law Robert Shawver is a title attorney in Dallas whose passion is real estate. He and my daughter Amy wanted to start a business, owning and managing residential real estate, and needed money to start. A model for this was done with some fabulously successful real estate companies in Houston. The young persons (Robert and Amy) have the vision and drive to do the business; the older persons (Joe and Linda) have money on which they would like to get a decent return.

Having access to readily available cash allows Robert to quickly buy properties, and Joe gets a reasonable return on his money and a share of the equity. Robert gets an equity return on his properties and doesn't have to put up money. This story has been repeated successfully many times in various businesses.

Furthermore, as part of growth and development, every business must have a long-term plan and vision. When a business first starts, the owner's objective often simply is to survive. Given the sobering statistics about the overall success of businesses, this is understandable. But it is true that a small enterprise must grow. It must grow to provide opportunities for employees, to provide encouragement for the owners, and to provide assurances to customers that it will be there to serve them. Employees want to know that they have a future with the company. The owners and their spouses and their banks need to have confidence that the business will be successful and sustainable. Customers need to believe that a company will be there to serve them in the future.

As the marketplace changes, these business plans and visions must continually adapt as well. At Stress, we did a from-scratch business plan every few years and updated it annually. The services that we offered to customers ten years ago are often no longer needed. And for us to be a viable supplier, we must constantly listen to customers and understand what services they will need in the next few years. We must acquire the technical skills and staff and business knowledge to serve those customers. If we don't do that, we'll be out of business.

When Stress was founded in 1972, the biggest service offering was providing certified stress reports for the many nuclear power plants under construction at the time. Today, we serve a wide variety of industries, ranging from oil and gas, plastics, pharmaceutical, medical devices, automotive, consumer products, aerospace, power and utilities, chemical and refinery, and pipeline. Over the years, our services continually changed as technology and clients' needs drove the business. We always listened to customers about their needs, and this resulted in more than eight hundred clients annually.

Sixth, consider this question, How should I share profits with partners and employees?

As the business grows and becomes successful, the owner will inevitably face questions of how to share the fruits of success. Many owners struggle with this, and successful owners do this in many different ways. My own belief was that the business would ultimately be more successful if benefits of the business were widely shared. That is why I believe that Stress Engineering has been recognized as one of the best places to work in Houston, Texas; New Orleans; and Cincinnati. And it is the reason we enjoyed very small turnover of employees—less than 3 percent annually for many years. When you evaluate the cost of hiring and training a competent employee, it is generally much cheaper to pay them well to keep them happy than to incur the costs and drain on management time in continually retraining new hires. Employee costs are generally two-thirds of all the costs of service businesses, so retention and productivity are both very important.

Seventh, after the hard work, ask yourself, What should my exit strategy be?

At the end of the day for a business, whatever that is, every business is either sold or goes out of business. Nothing, no one, lives forever. The owner should consider this from the start because it affects the strategy of ownership and how the business is run.

Many businesses owned by one or two people are designed to be sold to an acquiring company, and this is the typical exit strategy of business owners. If, however, the business owner's dream is to build a multigeneration family enterprise, then the critical element becomes whether or not a family member of the next generation is competent and capable to take over.

A consultant who became my friend was John Hoffmann, who owned and operated Safety Engineering Laboratories Inc. in Warren, Michigan. John has a PhD and was an expert in fires and explosions and also had a large, full-scale fire testing facility in upstate Michigan. We worked on a lot of investigations together, and I greatly respected him.

John's son, Don, started working in the business as a teenager and young engineer and liked it. He told his dad that he wanted to take over the business when John retired. John told him to do that, Don first had to get a PhD in chemical engineering and teach. Only with that background would he be qualified to run the company. So

Don did both and took over the company when John retired. As a result, the company has continued to prosper and is still one of the preeminent fire science companies in the nation. John also required a graduate degree for all engineers and helped pay for it. Stress had a similar policy for many years. Smart companies recognize the value of education for their employees and recognize that not only does this make more valuable employees but also more loyal employees.

Typically in professional practices, the practice is sold to a professional or group of professionals who want to take over the business. This is normal for doctors, dentists, and accountants. It is also very common for engineering companies. The problem with engineering companies, however, is that if they are successful, their value often grows too great for the next generation of professionals to afford to buy. This is why many engineering companies are sold to an acquirer at some point in their history.

In the case of Stress, we decided that the appropriate ownership transition strategy was an employee stock ownership program or ESOP. Using this strategy, the company is sold to the employees. Many engineering firms have done this, and some are large companies. Also, significant advantages in the US tax code encourage employee ownership through ESOPs. More than ten thousand ESOP companies now exist in the United States, and these are companies that regularly exhibit superior stability and financial performance. The key point of whether or not this is feasible in a given situation is whether the profitability of the company is sufficient to enable bank financing to be viable. Some ESOPs have failed when the company borrows too much to buy the shares of departing shareholders and then can't make the bank payments.

Eighth, ask yourself, how important are ethics?

Warren Buffet said that it takes twenty years to build a reputation and five minutes to ruin it. This is wisdom from one of the most successful investors ever.

Without ethics, it is almost impossible to have repeat customers. If you have to go win every customer new, your sales costs will be very high. Without ethics, it is impossible to have long-term employees in a free society. They won't work long-term for someone they do not respect. If employees don't work hard for you, your labor costs will be very high and your productivity will be very low. The most successful companies are run by ethical people.

Finally, consider this, How important is it to give back to the community?

John Wesley, the founder of the Methodist Church, is known for the famous quotation, "Make all you can, save all you can, give all you can." It seems to me that these words are closely tied to the concept of stewardship, where you manage something entrusted to you in a responsible way in order to pass it along to others.

One of the main reasons people are attracted to entrepreneurship is the possibility of making money. This is good and honorable. The second part of Wesley's quote is about saving. Any businessman who is successful long-term has developed the ability to do things efficiently and save money. This is necessary in both your personal life and your business life in order to have the privilege of continuing in business and in order to have the freedom to personally achieve the dreams of you and your family.

The third part of the quotation is sometimes harder for people to understand. It is a natural human attribute to want to leave the world a better place than you found it and to help those in need. This is a fundamental part of our culture. But one thing you may not have understood is how important it is for you yourself to give back to the community and the world. Someone who lives totally for oneself is not likely to have a happy life.

If you look at the huge number of people, for example, who give back to schools and institutions and the enormous amount of money they give, it certainly is not for their benefit. It's to make the world a better place for others, even strangers, and for those of us who come after them. And there are many, many worthy causes requiring stewardship.

I believe John Wesley had it right.

•

FOUR

The Strawberry Tub

As Told by Linda Fowler

The Strawberry Tub 1976

The namesake strawberry tub—an antique tin claw-foot bathtub that I hand painted mint green with red strawberries and their vining leaves—showcased our window overflowing with red strawberry-shaped soap. The tub was iconic, and the Strawberry Tub became the best-known card and gift shop in the Klein area of north Harris County, Texas.

After my older children were in school (Jodi and Rob) and Amy was big enough that she didn't need constant care, I was thinking of returning to work. I told Joe I wanted to get a job, and he suggested starting my own business. So I thought about it and decided that since I liked to shop and was a huge Hallmark fan, a card and gift store would be fun. And just think how much money I could save if I shopped at wholesale!

However, in 1976, when my sister and partner, Donna Picou, and I planned the store and took the lease at the intersection of Stuebner Airline and Louetta, diagonally across the street from Klein High School, the area was so sparsely developed that the Hallmark representative at first declined our location for lack of traffic in the area to support a Hallmark store. We went on with our planning and spent a week of selecting every card by hand that would go in our store for a whole year from a Hallmark competitor. Then the carpenter who was building the post office front inside the store told us that Hallmark was talking to another operator about opening a store in the same center—and that the potential operator had actually come inside that day to look around our premises!

I first talked to the landlord and reminded him of his contractual obligation not to lease to another card shop in the center. Then I talked to the area Hallmark location representative that I had been dealing with, who rechecked the traffic at the intersection of Stuebner Airline and Louetta and found there was enough traffic to open!

Since we already had a lease, Hallmark Cards (which really were the best-known and oldest brand) were finally added. The Strawberry Tub was in business as a Hallmark card and gift store. Hallmark's slogan "When you care enough to send the very best" made us strive to be the best in our business. This illustrates the type of difficulties all new start-ups experience, and successful entrepreneurs must have the drive and vision to overcome a number of obstacles.

"Business start-ups are notoriously hard, and retail is especially difficult with all its variables," said my husband, Joe. "My friends and partners weren't sure this was the best idea. But when you love somebody, and you suggested the idea in the first place, you want to

The Strawberry Tub

be supportive, and the Strawberry Tub was up and running." Always believe in yourself. If you don't, no one else will either.

We had a great deal of flexibility in choosing our stock, and we were able to do things that nobody else was doing at the time. For example, few gift shops ground coffee beans, fresh for taking home, or carried Russell Stover candy and truffles by the Sweet Shop for a sweet treat. A unique experience for the younger customers was the bead bar—where you could string your own one-of-a-kind necklace or bracelet while you waited—along with gourmet jelly beans by the pound and Hello Kitty gifts and collectiles. We added a floral shop so that the Klein high school students across the street could get their football mums onsite. We did floral wedding designs and sold wedding invitations to add to the full-service wedding offering.

We had a contract post office from the beginning so that shoppers could mail their purchases right then—without worrying about missing important dates—because the next nearest postal opportunity was seven miles away in Tomball. It was also a great help to increase foot traffic . . . one-stop shopping!

The Strawberry Tub Grand Reopening 1978. Pictured: Linda Asbill; Linda Fowler; Bernard Strack, Spring, Texas Postmaster; Donna Picou; Roby Armstrong, Hallmark Representative.

Introducing a new Precious Moments® figurine, cousins Amy Fowler and Jason Picou as the wedding cake topper.

As a special promotion for the opening of carrying Precious Moments porcelain figurines, Donna and I dressed up our own five- and six-year-olds as Precious Moments bride and groom to promote the collectibles taking center stage in the very popular line. During one open house promotion at the store, the mini bride and groom walked up and down the sidewalk outside and stood as wedding cake toppers on a faux bridal cake that was four feet tall.

The Strawberry Tub did all this and more, with the crowd-pulling merchandise sometimes bringing in a thousand customers in a single day. Some times were crazy, but it was fun. Even that first February when we realized that we were down to a few last Valentines a week before the actual day and had to rush to Foley's to replenish our stock—with theirs. About 40 percent of Valentines sales are made in the last two days of the holiday.

The Strawberry Tub

I can still hear the Foley's clerk as she rang up our huge stack of Valentines, saying, "Boy, you must have a lot of friends." We didn't make any profit on those cards bought at retail, but without them, we would have missed the gift sales that saw us through our first Valentine's Day. We kept learning and figuring out things and found ways to please our clientele that we enjoyed too.

The combination of many complementary lines that appealed to the same customer base meant that we had an extremely high individual average transaction (IAT), or sales per customer; and with a location that generated lots of customers, the Strawberry Tub was very profitable from the start. We were amazed at how rapidly sales increased. Also, we worked hard to always make our customers feel very important and welcome; we knew them by name, and we were part of the community.

The store opened with 1,300 square feet of retail space, enlarged to 3,300 square feet within two-and-a-half years, then enlarged again to 5,000 square feet with the floral shop addition and with our longtime friend Linda Asbill as a new partner. We would have two other shops, My Friends and Me that featured James Avery jewelry in Old Town Spring (before there were any stand-alone James Avery stores) and Thoughts N Things at Kuykendahl and FM 1960 (managed for part of its life by my brother-in-law John Picou), but the Strawberry Tub was the most productive and profitable.

The Strawberry Tub was my passion, and I instinctively knew that customer satisfaction was everything. Because it was a neighborhood store and carried such a broad product line, an average customer might visit three to four times a week.

We also had to be savvy businesswomen and carefully tracked the IAT. Having cards, lots of gifts, flowers, and candy really bumped up the IAT. So it was not hard to get the entire store sales to break even with basic card and a small number of gift sales, and then all the gross profit on additional sales dropped right to the bottom line. The store was always profitable, and having three stores reduced the overall corporate overhead per store. It was a thriving enterprise.

In the early years, Texas had blue laws that prohibited stores from opening on Sunday. Eventually, those were repealed; and since the overhead was already covered in the first six days of sales, Sunday afternoon was very profitable.

Donna, Linda Asbill, and I always kept up with the latest information and products from Hallmark and often went to buy the latest and cutest gifts at the Dallas Market. Lots of high school students—including our daughters and sons—got their first job at the Strawberry Tub, and all of them were trained in the right way to meet customer expectations from customer service to stocking the store to being able to spot shoplifters (yes, there were a few of those). Our children thought that having their mothers as the owners of the Strawberry Tub gave them a lot of social capital.

The floral staff was made up of professional designers, and the store did a booming business in weddings. Before the addition of the floral shop, I felt that I also needed to be educated in floral design. I completed design school in Houston and coursework at the Benz School of Floral Design at Texas A&M University. After passing certification, I became a licensed Texas master florist.

Valentine's Day became such a big business that a large eighteen-wheeler refrigerated truck was brought in to have enough space to hold all the inventory of flowers. One time, the temperature varied and the fifty arrangements on the floor of the truck froze and had to be redone . . . so much for getting ahead of the demand!

Ordering the correct amount of inventory for the seasonal business at Valentine's, Mother's Day, Thanksgiving, and Christmas was an expensive undertaking; and Joe's main contribution to helping was doing this tedious forecasting work. As the years went by, everyone became better and better at the overall business; and we stayed very busy selling, training store employees, finding new and fresh inventory of gifts, and promoting the business to the community. We loved it! The Strawberry Tub supported lots of little league baseball, soccer, and football teams in the area; and a large wall was covered with their team pictures.

Our customers were overwhelmingly women, except for Valentine's and Mother's Day when hordes of men would come in for a last-minute card or gift. They were not shopping—they were buying!

Over the years, a parallel prevailed as both the Strawberry Tub and Stress Engineering Services Inc. grew and prospered. Each company added services as needed, appealing to a growing number of customers while still serving the basic clientele. Joe and I listened to our customers. And by listening and responding to customers' expanding needs, our companies grew respectively.

By 1991, a lot of things were changing. The neighborhood grew significantly in the sixteen Christmases the Strawberry Tub had been open, and a lot of competitive businesses were attracted to the area. The post office built a local station nearby, and many drugstores and grocery stores were carrying Hallmark cards.

I had worked sixteen years with the busiest days of the year being Valentine's, Christmas Eve, and the day after Christmas (for half-price sales). Kids had grown up, graduated from college, gotten married; and our youngest, Amy, was a senior in high school. Two of the stores were sold to one operator in the late 1980s, and the Strawberry Tub was sold to another in 1991. It continued in operation under various owners until 2015—almost forty years.

Our retail businesses were great successes, always made good profits, and had lots of happy customers; and Linda, Donna, and I had a lot of fun! I continued for a number of years to use my Texas master florist skills to do special events and weddings. We still love retail though, and my sister Donna Picou and I have owned Jeanne's Monogramming & Gifts in Vintage Park, selling gifts and monogramming for the last ten years.

•

FIVE

Crafting Stress Engineering Services Inc.

When Stress Engineering Services Inc. was founded in 1972, the mission was to provide high-level engineering services to companies that occasionally needed the help of very technically competent professionals to solve difficult business problems. The founders were Harry Sweet, who had been a professor at Texas A&M University; Ray Latham, who had been the chief engineer at Gray Tool Company; and Joe Fowler, a young engineer with a PhD from Texas A&M who had two years' experience as a drilling research engineer at Texaco.

We each had significant strengths. Harry had been consulting for a number of years at A&M and was relatively well known; Ray had very good knowledge of the nuclear power market, which Gray served; and I had a first-rate education in numerical analysis and modeling of physical systems as well as a good understanding of drilling problems from my time at Texaco. While a PhD student, I had helped Harry and Pete Weiner, another professor at A&M, in their consulting businesses and had truly enjoyed the work, the challenge of hard problems, and the satisfaction of really helping a client.

Crafting Stress Engineering Services Inc.

Ray Latham and Joe Fowler working on a hydraulic pump, c. 1973.

At the beginning, the biggest service offering was providing certified stress reports for the many nuclear power plants under construction. This was a sound business since every nuclear plant had to have a stress report for every component in the facility (thousands of reports). Ray Latham had the contacts to secure the work, and very few firms had the capability to do these reports.

This was a fundamental business until 1979, when the Three Mile Island nuclear power plant suffered a loss of reactor coolant accident, and there was a partial meltdown of the reactor core. Concern about nuclear safety basically ceased plant construction and the need for these stress reports. Our company had to find new business, and fortunately, we had begun a new service offering of the company a few years earlier.

Stress had started work for the offshore drilling and production industry and developed the first commercial software to design and analyze marine risers. These are the pipes that go from the drilling platform to the ocean floor and allow drilling and production operations to be safely conducted. Risers are subject to waves and currents and are very sensitive to the tension that is maintained on them. I had learned how to numerically model these types of systems in my PhD work and thus was able to secure an important project to develop modeling software that enabled our manufacturing company client to properly design the risers they manufactured.

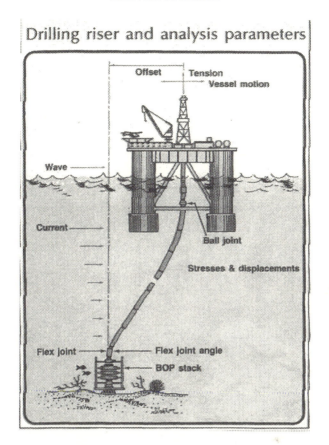

Used for marine riser program; oil and gas industry and subsea mining working on the ocean floor.

We were fortunate to secure the services of Ron Young, another young PhD with experience in modeling car crashes, and he and I were the primary authors of this work. Riser design and analysis became a strong specialty of Stress, and it continues as an important business area to this day. In addition to Ron, Chuck Miller, John Chappell, and Allen Fox were instrumental in this work. And for this work, Ron, Allen, and I were inducted into the Offshore Energy Center Technology Hall of Fame in 2014.

Also, we began the development of an independent third-party test laboratory. This enabled us to provide performance testing of full-scale components like casing, riser, and tubing connections and all manner of equipment. An analysis is good, but a test is the real proof of fitness for purpose. Tom Asbill was the driving force behind this business. The instrumentation skills we had to develop to control these tests could also be applied to real equipment in the field. Jim Albert was our first electrical engineer, and he, too, was crucial for this work.

What's in a Name?

Three of us founded our company in 1972—Harry Sweet, Ray Latham, and Joe Fowler. So like a lot of entrepreneurs, we named the firm after ourselves—Sweet, Latham, and Fowler. About two years later, Ray decided that he truly wanted a manufacturing company and left our firm to establish Reflange Inc., which became a successful manufacturer.

Harry Sweet was then the majority partner, and the company became Harry Sweet & Associates. We continued under that name and grew some until 1983 when a combination of events caused another name change. First, we started into a downturn in the upstream business. Second, it was clear to most of the partners that we would need to make significant investments in our computer systems and into our lab test business, both of which were doing well. Harry was uncomfortable doing that as well as handling the increased management roles of a bigger company. He resigned in order to return to the business of consulting where he was comfortable.

It was clear that we would have another name change. But what name? In a consulting business, clients tend to identify with the individual service provider who services them. But if the company grows significantly, soon there are too many names in the firm to accommodate everyone. Also, as the firm grows and takes on new principals or partners, their names not being in the company name may divide, rather than unite, the partners. Given that our goal from the start was to have a company where internal cooperation was paramount, we decided that a far better solution long-term was to have a company name that did not include any individual's name.

But what name?

Two factors influenced our decision. First, we conferred with a well-known naming consultant about the importance of a name to the success of a company. He confided that it really didn't make much difference as long as you stuck to the name and continuously promoted it. Second, in 1972, Exxon was adopted as the single name of all the Standard Oil of New Jersey company names—Esso, Enco, Humble, etc. If the largest oil company could change their name without affecting their business, why couldn't we?

So we asked for suggestions from employees and received a number of them. We finally settled on Stress Engineering Services Inc. as our new name in 1984. The name is related to all the practice areas in which we practice; it's easy to remember, and it has worked!

For all the nonengineering types reading this, *stress* is a term that defines the force per unit area going through a structure. For instance, if a bar one inch in diameter is holding up one thousand pounds, the stress in the bar is calculated as one thousand pounds divided by 0.7854 square inches (the cross-sectional area of the bar), which equals 1,273 pounds per square inch or psi. That stress can be compared with the material strength of the bar to see if it will fail. In layman's terms, material strength means the amount of stress that a material is able to sustain before it fails.

Continued Development of Stress

Basic mathematical modeling of equipment was a key component of our services from the start. Finite element analysis (FEA) is a computer prediction of stresses and deflections in complicated equipment, and we used it from the beginning of the company in all industries. We were one of the earliest commercial service providers of this type of work in the country. We also used our basic engineering skills to provide independent analyses of moving equipment such as cranes, riser tensioners, and basic fluid dynamics problems. Jack Miller and Randy Long were instrumental in this work. But the test lab continued to grow and really took off after we bought a thirty-three-thousand-square-foot building out of foreclosure in 1986. Having the ability to do both analyses and tests, either in the lab or the field, was a huge competitive advantage. Comparison of the two methods on the same part or structure enabled us to provide clients with unparalleled speed and quality to the development of safe equipment. Along with Tom Asbill, Bob Wink was also instrumental in this success.

When we started the company, we did our computer analysis on mainframe computers where we bought time by the minute. This was very expensive. In the mid-1980s, we bought our first minicomputer to do this work in-house. This greatly improved our response time and helped control costs. Allen Fox managed our computer systems.

In-house computers affected our business as well because many customers began to do FEA themselves in-house. As the business changed, this resulted in another major change in our services. We became more overall problem solvers and used our analyses and testing skills to advise major oil companies on the safety of the equipment they operated or considered buying. This was good as the problems we targeted were larger, and we really had no effective competition.

But by the mid-to-late 1980s, business in Houston in the upstream oil business became very slow as low oil prices negatively affected our upstream manufacturing and oil company customers. Once more, we responded by looking elsewhere for work and began working in the refinery, chemical, and pipeline businesses. These were relatively easy transitions since all our technical skills were directly transferable. Richard Boswell was the pioneer in our coke drum work, and when Bobby Wright came into the company a few years later, this work really took off. Coke drums are large steel pressure vessels used at the end of the crude oil refining process to extract the last and heaviest hydrocarbons. They are subject to cyclic internal pressure and high temperatures, which make them susceptible to cracking and failure.

In Proverbs, it says, "A man skillful in his work will stand before kings." That certainly proved true in our history because one of our software suppliers who knew of our skills in finite element analysis recommended us to another customer of theirs—a huge supplier of consumer products. Our analysis and design work on packaging saved that customer many millions of dollars. This also resulted in work for ten to fifteen employees that continued for many years and is the reason we have a Cincinnati office since our client P&G asked us to open an office there in 1992. We were fortunate to get our first client in consumer products, Clint Haynes, to lead this work. He became the vice president of Stress and continues to be a visionary in consumer and medical products consulting.

At that time, 1992, I used outside metallurgists for my own projects so much that we realized we could hire one full time. Not only would this be a good source of revenue, it would also jumpstart our failure analysis business since most clients automatically call a metallurgist when they have a failure. This is true even if the failure has nothing to do with materials.

We thought taking a broader multidisciplinary approach to failures would result in a better service, and that certainly proved true. Paul Kovach was our first metallurgist, followed by Ken Riggs and Kim Flesner. Kim took over leading the practice, and we grew to forty people doing that type of work. Materials engineering is very important.

Our labs and business continued to grow throughout the '90s, and in 1999, we purchased a competitor of our testing business, H. O. Mohr Research & Engineering. Jack Miller took over managing that business and did a great job integrating it into our culture and making it very profitable.

Development of Practices

I have mentioned offshore design and analysis, test labs, consumer products, instrumentation, and material engineering as separate service competencies that naturally developed at Stress. We began to realize the significant marketing and operational advantages to structuring our business around these practices. First, clients began to think of our company as the place to go for each of our practice areas. As professionals in a practice area got busy, it was natural to hire and train young engineers and technicians in that area. However, many young engineers could be trained to be proficient in multiple practice areas. And as the company grew, it also was natural to make the leaders in each of these areas principals, or owners, in the company. This is similar to the type of organizations that develop in the legal, accounting, and medical professions. It enables competent professionals to share work and take vacations!

Another major reason for the development of practices is the realization that the problems that clients ask for help on are hard. If the problems were easy, clients would do them themselves. Essentially, every engineering challenge is truly interdisciplinary. The example that was the "aha" for our metallurgy practice was that, as said earlier, almost all clients will call a metallurgist when they have a failure. Yet very often, the cause of the failure has nothing to do with metallurgy but is rather the result of an operational or design problem. A third reason is that the company became known as the expert in many niches in many industries. Our experts relate to the problems in each industry and became the go-to people for that industry. This is reinforced by participation in industry committees in many industries. This process is how Stress came to have so many clients and experienced rapid growth for many years.

Getting the right answer involves getting the experts who can address these issues involved. As it also says in Proverbs, "Plans fail for lack of counsel, but with many advisors, they succeed." So having different disciplines to collaborate on a common problem almost always results in a better answer.

As the company grew throughout the last forty-plus years, other practices like pipeline engineering; refinery and chemical plant engineering; medical device development; and plant engineering, procurement, and construction (EPC) developed. This process will continue for the life of the company as industries and customer needs continually change. But at Stress, the goal of each of our practices has always been to be the best in the world in each of the disciplines and specialties we offer.

Test Laboratories and Threaded Pipe Connections

Our test labs have been a major competitive advantage for Stress since Tom Asbill led the opening of our first one in 1978. The ability to analyze equipment is great, but to have the ability to prove equipment integrity through a test is a very necessary function for our clients who manufacture and use equipment. When we bought our first building in 1986, the main attraction was that it had a large laboratory space; and from the beginning, it really helped our business.

Harvest of Riches

The H. O. Mohr business we bought in 1999 was primarily a testing business. After it was clear it would be successful, we built an office-lab facility near our original building and ran the two labs in a coordinated fashion. After a number of years, the business grew to the point where we desperately needed more space. Randy Long found a ninety-two-acre tract near Waller, Texas, that was only about thirty miles from our Houston office. We bought that land, and it has been the central growth mechanism for our lab business. We have built four large test buildings at that facility. Randy has continued to do a magnificent job of leading this laboratory practice and leads it today.

Overall, Stress Engineering Services Inc. laboratories encompass more than 130,000 square feet of mostly high-bay laboratories in eight different facilities, housing an extensive array of testing equipment to test production and prototype equipment for the following:

- Loads ranges of ten million pounds to a fraction of an ounce
- Pressures to sixty thousand psi internal and thirty thousand psi external
- Temperatures from -300 °F (liquid nitrogen) to 1,500 °F
- Special flow tests of equipment from miniature to full-scale fatigue and vibration testing
- Testing with H_2S (hydrogen sulfide), CO_2 (carbon dioxide), and other special gases
- A large variety of specialized fixtures to hold test specimens

These are major pieces of equipment representing many millions of dollars of investment over a long period. Some were built with Stress investment dollars, and a number were paid for by the projects that needed the specialized testing performed.

Steve Kinyon of our Waller lab provided this insight: "Some of the most difficult engineering performed at Stress often involves how to safely conduct large-scale equipment tests to representative service conditions through failure. This requires extreme dedication to safety by everyone involved, and the ability to numerically simulate very difficult conditions. For example, pressurizing a twenty-four-inch-diameter pipeline section to failure using a medium like high-temperature water (changes to steam) or liquid carbon dioxide that changes from liquid to gas when the failure occurs, is one type of high-energy tests Stress performs."

Steve continued, "Stress performed a series of these types of tests on a simulated pipeline to examine the effectiveness of devices used in pipelines designed to arrest cracks, which can run the full length of the pipeline without the protection of the arrestors. A fracture in a high-pressure carbon dioxide pipeline is one condition where arrestors may be beneficial.

"Carbon dioxide is a liquid for all practical purposes when pressurized above 1,100 psi, depending on the temperature. When fracture occurs in a liquid CO_2 transmission pipeline, the transition from liquid to gas can occur at a pressure that is high enough to maintain and grow the crack down the entire length of the pipe; the crack tip is continuously subjected to pressure from the liquid phase inside the pipe, which changes to gas after the crack passes it. The event of releasing the liquid into gas media is extremely energetic on this scale and is completed in milliseconds." Steve is truly an expert in large-scale potentially hazardous testing, and each test of this type is subjected to a multiexpert, rigorous review process.

A large part of our test work involves the threaded pipe connections that are used to screw together thirty-foot- to fifty-foot-long joints of pipe used to drill wells (drill pipe) and complete wells (casing and tubing). These connections can be from two and one-half inches to forty-eight inches in diameter and, in fact, are very complicated structures. The connections have to structurally withstand high-tension (stretching) loads, high-torsional (twisting) loads, and high-bending (weight from doglegs or sharp bends in the hole) loads without failing. Not only do they have to maintain structural integrity, they also have to remain leak tight with zero leakage. And they have to do this under temperatures that can reach four hundred degrees or hotter and in the presence of very corrosive chemicals.

Cross section of the threaded pipe connection used in oil and gas service.
Image courtesy of JFE Steel

For example, a twenty-thousand-foot-long string of pipe may have five hundred connections; and for safety, not one of them can leak! This means, the reliability of these connections has to be extremely high, and each connection may have to withstand many different combinations of operating loads and temperatures. Moreover, a product line of a particular connection design may have many dozens of combinations of size, pressure and tension rating (thickness requirements), and material. So the number of different connections that have to be qualified, meaning proven for service, is very large. Furthermore, an operator well owner can't afford to take the risk that any of the connections will leak. Generally, the supplier of the connections pays for the required testing, and having a respected third-party laboratory like Stress doing the testing gives credibility to the whole process. Stress's clients are generally the connection supplier or the oil company operator if they want independent proof that a particular design is acceptable.

These connections are extremely critical and difficult to make properly. The threads of the connection are very shallow, which means that they are easy to cross-thread and are very susceptible to "jumping out" of engagement under load. These types of threads are necessary because several strings (attached joints) of casing and tubing have to fit inside the hole making up the well. Large holes are very expensive so the holes are drilled as small in diameter as possible. The design of connections to fit inside them is very precise. The wellbore holes truly represent extremely expensive real estate.

For Stress, this testing and evaluation is a very good business. A lot of credit has to be given to Tom Asbill, our partner who was a pioneer in all this work. For many years, he worked with the committees of operators and manufacturers who wrote the test standards, and his friendships with the major clients and his training of our testing staff were instrumental to the development of this business.

This work to qualify connections has made the industry far safer. Historically, many blowouts, failures, and deaths were the result of failed pipe-threaded connections.

Floating Systems Design and Analysis

Earlier, I described the development of marine riser analysis software that was important to the founding of the company. This software developed into our floating systems practice that has been the largest practice in the company for many years. Offshore failures are so expensive that preventing them is critically important to the clients who are mainly the major offshore operators like Shell, Chevron, Exxon, British Petroleum, and others; the equipment suppliers; and the drilling contractors who actually drill the offshore wells.

The original riser software was called DERP (damned efficient riser program). It basically analyzed, with small deflection theory in two dimensions, a riser pipe that was loaded by waves, currents, and prescribed ship motions. In the early 2000s, John Chappell and David Garrett headed up a Stress-funded multimillion dollar project to develop a modern software that considered much more complicated systems. It modeled combined floaters and multiple pipes in three dimensions and handled the random nature of sea states, currents, and vessel motions (which it calculated). This was, and is, a state-of-the-art software as good as any in the world. It is called RAMS (rational analysis of marine systems).

Our work usually starts with exploratory drilling. We help the clients select a rig that is suitable for the project and help them develop operating criteria, like the sea state (wind, waves, and current) that is limiting for the location and vessel, and critical operating decisions such as how much tension to pull on the riser systems. Often we supply the clients with real-time operating software that they can use either on the rig or at the office. The work may be done for the operating company, the drilling or pipeline contractor, or all of them.

Once a discovery is made, we often help clients design the facilities and methods of production. In water depths up to about one thousand foot deep, historically, this could be a rigid bottom-founded structure. In deeper water, a facility that moves with the ocean is needed since rigid bottom-founded structures are not feasible. This is because shallow water platforms are designed as rigid frame structures that resist movement and shear due to wind, waves, and current by basic tension and compression loads in the bracing and columns of the structures. These require very deep and strong piles to carry the load to the ground. At some water depth, this becomes too difficult and expensive to be practical. Examples for deeper water facilities are tension leg platforms (TLP), ship-shaped floaters, or semisubmersible platforms that have various shapes. The TLPs are moored by the legs, and the other two are moored by mooring lines. Deeper water structures accommodate their loads by allowing relatively large lateral movements of the structures.

By the way, the polyester mooring lines used in deepwater drilling have been extensively developed, tested, and qualified at Stress Engineering Services Inc. Ray Ayers and Cesar del Vecchio of Stress won numerous awards for this work. Without polyester mooring, deepwater floating production facilities would not be feasible. The design of the offshore facility also includes the pipelines. The lines have to get from the floater to the ocean floor, and this design work also utilizes our engineers and our RAMS software. There are many possible configurations, and selection of the best is an intensive engineering effort.

One main purpose of the offshore facility is to separate the oil, gas, and water produced by the well; reinject the water; then ship the oil and gas to shore. Today, many new projects use subsea separation, and all these functions are remotely done without bringing the produced fluids to the surface. The facilities are different but still require the knowledge and calculation skills of engineers like those at Stress to assure success and safety. The subsea equipment requires very high levels of reliability, and Stress's labs often assist with this work.

Electrical and Instrumentation Engineering

Our first electrical engineer in 1985 was Jim Albert. He started helping us after we had some problem with instrumentation projects that resulted from Tom Asbill and me trying to do electrical engineering work when we weren't electrical engineers. The worst example was when we tried to measure the stresses in a large vertical reactor (over one hundred foot tall) being lifted by Brown & Root at a Houston-area process plant.

We got the project at the last minute and had to spend three days and nights—straight—laying and wiring up strain gauges before the big lift. To make the schedule, Tom had the bright idea that we would use a common ground for each bank of ten gauges and save the time of running individual wires to each gauge. An electrical engineer would have known common wiring is a no-no and would result in none of the gauges working. When the vessel was lifted, the gauges all drifted so much, we got no useful data. The client was very upset since we got no data, and we had to eat the entire cost of the job. We realized we really needed electrical engineering help!

Jim helped us first as a contractor. His first project, I remember, was instrumenting a long-stroke pumping unit we were developing to replace the conventional horsehead oil well-pumping unit. Long stroke with a vertical stroke can have strokes thirty feet or more and can be much more efficient since they are less troubled by sucker rod dynamics than conventional rotational horsehead units. Jim drove a big station wagon that seemed like it had every tool and part known to man in the back. He would drive anywhere, anytime, to the field to fix the instrumentation and controls on the prototype units. He was a magician!

After Jim joined us, we realized what a rare find we really had. One project was trying to figure out what was causing a severe vibration at a parking garage at 601 Travis in downtown Houston. This was a twenty-story parking garage for Texas Commerce Bank, now Chase Bank. The building covered an entire city block and had parking on the lower fifteen floors and offices above with the Texas Club, a health club, on the top floor. At certain times of the day, the building shook so badly it would jostle coffee out of your cup on the fifteenth floor, where the bank's entire computer network was housed. Naturally, the vibration affected the data storage units.

There were lots of theories as to the cause, such as wind or cars driving up or down and so forth, but we proposed to the building manager to instrument the building and monitor the vibration for a day to find the cause. Jim brought the accelerometers and recorders, and the data collection began. About midafternoon, the whole building began to shake severely. We traced the cause to an aerobics dance class of one-hundred-plus women dancing in unison in the large gym in the health club. Concentrated and rhythmic energy from the dancers was imparted to the gym floor and down the concrete columns of the building to the floors below. After the cause was understood, an easy fix was to separate the dancers into smaller groups in different rooms, which cured the problem.

Another project was to diagnose the cause of severe vibrations from an elevated, partially liquid-filled evaporator structure at a plant in McIntosh, Alabama. It was more than five hundred miles from Houston, and the project required a lot of equipment. Jim and I didn't want to drive that far, so we got one of our technicians to drive the company van to Mobile, where we flew to meet him and the van.

The technician had taken the van first to Florida to meet friends, and after we met him, he flew back to Houston. When we arrived at the plant, the guard asked if we had any alcohol, guns, or cameras in the van; and we said no since we hadn't packed any. Well, he searched the van and found all three left in the van by our technician!

We explained what had happened and went on and did the project, which was a great success because of Jim. He was able to wire our vibration monitoring into the control system of the plant. By running a few simple tests, the plant determined what operating conditions (flow, pressure, etc.) caused the vibrations, and they were able to completely avoid them with some minor process adjustments. A big success!

Jim Albert is a true pioneer in the business of taking and using real data to solve customers' hardest technical problems. Clients want specific, understandable data that is directly useful for their operations. This is a central "aha" of all our field service and measurement work.

Litigation Support, Expert Witness, and Disaster Recovery Work

Since early in the company's history, we did litigation support and expert testimony; and that work eventually grew into providing management services for large disasters like plant fires, pipeline failures, and blowouts. That work involves documenting evidence and helping the facility restart operations safely as soon as possible. For many of us, this was interesting work because the cases usually tested the limits of what was good design and engineering practice, and those of us who experienced it became better engineers as a result. Kim Flesner is truly a world-class expert at evidence management after a major disaster.

In the 1990s, the work grew to the extent that in some years it represented 10 percent of the company's work. We charged much higher prices because the work was demanding and interrupted our normal work and because the legal industry tended to be slow-paying clients. Our clients were the companies that had been sued, or the companies suing them, or the insurance companies. Personally, I testified more than eighty times, either by deposition or in trial, about half of the time for the defendants and half time for the plaintiffs.

An expert's job is to provide reliable expert opinions about the cause or causes of an accident or loss. The court uses this to help settle the matter. Everyone wants a competent expert who can clearly explain complicated engineering matters to lay juries and one who would support their version of the cause, or causes, of the failure or loss.

At Stress, we would examine the matter and then give our client our opinion of the causes of the failure or loss. If our opinion supported the client's theory of the case, they often called us to testify. If they did not like our opinion, they paid us, and the matter would be over for us. Therefore, when we actually testified, we could state our opinions clearly and with conviction.

After participating in approximately thirty trials, I came to appreciate that there are a lot of variables in a trial—among them the competence of the attorneys for each side, the strength of the evidence, impartiality of the judge, and the most unpredictable and significant variable: the jury. Most of the time, the side I testified for won, but I came to realize that the experts are not the most important variable in who actually prevails.

It was clear to me that the legal process can be uncertain, expensive, complicated, and demanding. As the business leader of Stress, I always endeavored to manage our business so that we did not get sued or have to sue anyone else. This meant listening to clients, reading contracts, checking clients' credit, having a good-quality assurance system for the work, and working safely. I am proud that we never had to defend or prosecute a significant lawsuit throughout my entire time as president, during which we served well over ten thousand clients across my career.

As the company grew to have such a large number of clients, it became more and more difficult to continue litigation support work. Our policy was that we would never take a case that was adverse to an existing client. However, almost every large company in Houston involved in the energy industry was an existing client; so as a result over the years, we have done less and less of this type of work, with one exception.

With a major accident like a refinery fire or a pipeline explosion, clients have a strong need to immediately have competent staff available to preserve evidence and to provide expeditious engineering guidance to the steps needed to restart operations. This has become a strong business for Stress, and it is not uncommon for billings from these assignments to be several million dollars.

The Water Heater Wars

In 1992, I was asked to investigate the circumstances of a water heater fire in Houston that left two small children seriously burned. Over the next fifteen years, I testified in twenty-one cases that were all similar, and Stress built laboratory recreations of more than ten of these. Our great laboratory staff, headed by Mark Cooper, became experts in building exact replicas of accident scenes and events and demonstrating the principles about which I and other experts would testify.

Test showing ignition of gasoline vapors from a floor-mounted water heater and the movement of the flame front back to the spilled gasoline from the water heater on the left. Typical victims would be standing where the gasoline can is on the far right

These cases all involved gas-fired water heaters sitting on the floor in a garage or, occasionally, in another room in the house. The water heaters, usually called hot water heaters in the South, take their air for combustion from floor-level openings in the heater for the burners that are about two inches off the floor. If gasoline is spilled on the floor nearby, some of it vaporizes and makes a vapor about three times as heavy as air that stays near the ground. When the water heater turns on and the burners start (or to a lesser extent from the always-on pilot light), the gasoline vapors can be pulled into the water heater if the spill is nearby (maybe within ten to fifteen feet of the heater). When the gasoline vapors go into the heater, they ignite and flash back to the original gasoline spill, making an instant fire in the pool of liquid gasoline. This pool was usually where the children were standing, which is why the burns were typically very severe.

Unfortunately, until the design was fixed in 2003, the cause of the spill in many of the fires was often a child (usually a three-to-five-year-old boy) trying to imitate his dad and filling the lawn mower with gasoline, which was usually stored in the garage. When a spill happened, the child was often caught right in the middle of a bad pool fire, resulting in very serious injuries or worse.

The Consumer Product Safety Commission (CPSC) found in the ten-year period (1985–1994) that an average of 260 serious fire injuries and twenty deaths occurred *each year* from this type of accident!

As a group, the water heater manufacturers did not take any responsibility for these injuries and deaths. They were sued many times, and their standard defenses were below:

- Their product did not cause the fire; gasoline did.
- The cause of the accidents were parents not properly supervising their children.

The plaintiffs' attorneys representing the victims and the experts they employed, including me, argued that it is the duty of a manufacturer to design their product to anticipate foreseeable misuse of a product and to provide safeguards in the design of the product to preclude injury. Ed Downing, an attorney from Metairie, Louisiana, made presentations to both the water heater manufacturer design committee and the CPSC and deserves thanks for that.

Our testing showed that if the water heater was elevated eighteen inches off the ground, the accidents would practically never happen, and all the manufacturers would have to do was ship an eighteen-inch stand with each water heater. This works because of the density difference between air and gasoline vapors. As mentioned, gasoline vapors are three times as heavy as air. At an elevation of eighteen inches off the ground, the gasoline vapors do not support combustion because the concentration of gasoline vapor is below the lower combustion limit, meaning the mixture is too lean to burn.

This war between the water heater manufacturers on one side and the victims and their attorneys on the other and the horrible burns and deaths to children continued on for more than ten years after I first became involved. In 2003, in an attempt to pressure the CPSC to order the water heaters manufacturers to ship a stand with every heater, Dr. John Hoffmann, his associates, and I published a refereed journal paper documenting the science of elevation and urging action.

Finally, also in 2003, the national water heater codes were changed to require new water heaters to be flammable vapor ignition resistant (FVIR). These codes were published by the American National Standards Institute (ANSI Z211.10 / CSA 4). After 2003, gas-fired residential water heaters must be designed to accommodate the foreseeable misuse of gasoline being spilled in their vicinity without a resulting fire. This standard was achieved by using sealed combustion chambers and flame arresters on the air intake.

We (the plaintiff expert community) suggested this technology many times, and the manufacturer response was always that it was too expensive. Yet flame arresters had been invented by Sir Humphry Davy in 1815 to provide protection from accidental ignition from miner's lamps in underground mines when gas was present, so it was not new technology. Flame arresters work by slowing down the products of combustion that try to escape the flame by forcing them to go through a screen on the way out. This cools them off enough where they will not ignite the gasoline vapors away from the fire.

I have often pondered why the manufacturers were unwilling to take responsibility for the safety of their products for so long. Thousands of people were burned and hundreds died because of their attitude. I believe it is the responsibility of people in business to really think about their ethical responsibilities in their work and to do the right thing even if it seems hard or expensive. I believe it starts and ends with the attitude of the engineers and managers in control.

Engineers should learn and should know that the hierarchy of design is to first identify the hazard and, hopefully, design it out of the product. If that cannot be done, the possibility of harm from the hazard should be reduced through engineering or process design/control. Only if those two items don't work, then the consumer should be warned or other means be used to reduce the hazard.

Research Projects

Much of the work of Stress, particularly in our laboratories, has actually been applied research projects. As I looked over my publications list, I saw publications about the following topics:

- Fire safety of bolted connections—will they leak in a fire?
- How connections withstand combined loads (i.e., pressure, twisting, and tension/compression)
- Collapse behavior of submerged pipelines
- Effects of dents on subsequent life of pipelines

Stress has done many other major research projects on a variety of topics important to the industry. Sponsors are typically organizations like the American Petroleum Institute (API); the Pipeline Research Council International (PRCI); DeepStar, an oil company group; or in some cases, agencies of the federal government. One of my pipeline collapse papers (with Carl Langner of Shell) won the 2015 American Society of Civil Engineers Hall of Fame Award as one of the most significant papers of the last twenty years. The paper gave designers practical advice for designing deepwater pipelines. Chris Alexander was an important contributor to the pipeline dent work and continued to do significant research in that field after I left.

Consumer Products Services

Starting in the late 1980s, Stress Engineering Services Inc. began conducting detailed design and analysis on consumer products. This accelerated when Clint Haynes joined Stress in 1992 and rapidly spread to medical products as well. One of the greatest successes was a project that won a prestigious AmeriStar Award from the Institute for Packaging Professionals, told by Clint Haynes and Mike Swindeman of the Stress Cincinnati office: "When it comes to consumer products, packaging is always one of the most important considerations, and as far as selling water goes, packaging is almost the only consideration there is. The story of the Aquafina bottle that changed the industry is a story of when a structural design problem crossed the threshold into art or as close as a packaging engineer is ever likely to get.

"Pepsi approached Stress with the desire to make a lightweight bottle. Lightweight bottles are less expensive because they use less material, and because they use less material, they are also eco-friendly. Unfortunately, to the consumer, eco-friendly and inexpensive translate to cheap with all the negative connotations. So Pepsi not only wanted lightweight but wanted to maintain the appearance and feel of a heavy bottle. Then they added one more constraint: Pepsi wanted to make a design that could someday be used for lightly carbonated beverages.

"Normally, having circumferential ribs would be an obvious choice to stiffen the shell, but circumferential ribs are a rather poor choice for pressurized containers because they tend to expand. Moreover, when top-loaded in pallets, circumferential ribs are a negative because they buckle very easily. So Stress came up with the idea of a segmented rib design. The design process was actually fairly simple. We parameterized the rib segments in terms of their length, depth, and spacing and ran a series of finite element models for bottles under squeeze, pressure, and top-load conditions. Two designs stood out, and we offered them both: a short rib pattern called Super Rib 1 and a long rib pattern called Super Rib 2. Both maintained the squeeze stiffness and had adequate top-load capabilities, retaining their shape under pressure. But Super Rib 1 was just a little more visually attractive. Hence the long rib pattern lost out, and Super Rib 1 became simply Super Rib.

"When the first prototypes were made, Super Rib bottles had such a pleasant aesthetic that the Pepsi folks decided the consumer would love to see the design in the water bottle. The Pepsi labeling team worked hard to invent a clear light-blue label through which the rib pattern produced a shimmering, wavy appearance. The combination of bottle design and labeling garnered the Aquafina water bottle the Institute of Packaging Professional's AmeriStar Award in 2003. After the new bottles hit the market, the super rib design was quickly copied by other bottlers, including rival Coca-Cola's Dasani brand. In just a few years, labeled, ribbed clear plastic water bottles had pushed their predecessors off the shelves and into the recycling bins of history.

"As a note, Pepsi kept experimenting with design, even producing a bottom-to-top version of the super rib bottle that resembled an art deco flower vase. The super rib success also led to other new attempts to produce sculptured plastic containers, many of which became projects at SES."

Award-winning water bottle design.

Sales and Marketing

The nature of the consulting business is that clients will have a problem and desperately need us until the problem is diagnosed (our work) and fixed (their work). After that, they may not need us for a considerable period. Thus, it is necessary for the growth of the business to continually find new clients.

Up until 1991, our engineers did all the work of finding new clients. That year, we hired our first professional marketing person, Terry Lechinger. Historically, most of our marketing had been person to person; and that required people who were skilled at finding potential customers, meeting them, and developing a relationship with them so the customers were comfortable with us. Most engineers are not blessed with this natural skill, but the sales professionals are.

If we leave actual customers happy with us and our work, it is natural that they or their company will call us the next time they have a problem, and over 80 percent of our work comes that way. But without the marketing people, it would be very difficult for our company to grow. And today, indirect marketing through websites and social media is becoming more and more important, especially for our younger clients. Our sales and marketing staff, still led by Terry Lechinger, has done a great job in this area (see www.stress.com). Alan Carlock has become a true expert in social media marketing.

After we reserved and started promoting our website name in the early 1990s, we had an irate lady call us and complain that we should donate that name to the public because when people are under stress and need help, that is a logical name for them to look under. We replied that our clients need help too!

Customers

Over the years, our services continually evolved as technology and clients' needs drove the business. We always listened to customers about their needs, and this resulted in more than eight hundred clients annually. Many of them are Fortune 500 companies who have been clients almost since the beginning of the company. These large customers have also been marketing challenges at times. This is because there are literally hundreds of potential individual customers within large international companies. Terry came up with the idea of customer forums to address this problem and to also make sure we understand where these customers are going and what they think their future needs will be.

When you get knowledgeable representatives from four to eight large companies together, generally, they will be open about their plans and needs as long as the subject does not go to competitive areas for them—like reservoir productivity for oil companies for example. Much of our work was driven by the need to address potential safety problems, new materials, and better operational procedures.

As Stress grew larger, and we were doing 2,500 projects a year for eight hundred customers, control of the projects and customer feedback became more difficult. By the mid-2000s, we had a feedback system that queried each customer after a project. This has become the standard for most companies today, and things like a net promoter score provide good guidance on how well we are doing and let us know about any unhappy customers so that we can immediately address an issue. The net promoter score is calculated by first asking customers to rate how likely they are to use your services from 1 to 10. Then the percentage of 0–6 respondents is subtracted from the percentage of 9–10 respondents. The result is your net promoter score. Doing these surveys by email has greatly simplified the process.

In the long term, the most important success metrics for our company (and, indeed, any company) truly are customer satisfaction and employee satisfaction. Success with both is required for Stress, or any company, to be successful. Employee satisfaction is actually more important because employee satisfaction, proper project manager training, and adequate company resources for the project manager lead directly to client satisfaction.

As our company grew, we had employee project manager training for many years, and the people who were good project managers were very important to the company (and generally the best paid). The sometimes-difficult activities of managing work scopes, budgets, and schedules have to be done well for the customer to be happy.

Company Culture

Company culture is absolutely crucial. It drives everything. As Peter Drucker is attributed with the saying, "Culture eats strategy for breakfast." This is so true. At Stress, we had a very good company culture during most of my time as president. Good culture results in happy customers, employees and leaders working together, people wanting to come to work in the morning, happy employees, low employee turnover, and good financial results for the company. Bad culture results in gossiping, strife at work, employees afraid of or distrustful of leaders, people not enjoying coming to work, unhappy customers because everyone is not pulling as a team to please clients, much-expensive turnover of employees, poor financial results, and, typically, a short company life span. Of course, the basic market for your services is very important also, but poor culture is a killer for a company.

As president, for many years, I taught our employees that the success factors for Stress Engineering Services Inc. were as follows:

1. Technical excellence
2. Client service
3. Right stuff on time
4. Internal cooperation

Really, number 3 is a combination of numbers 1 and 2. But over the years, we realized that our culture was far richer than just these four factors. In 2010, when we were adding forty to fifty people per year, we were looking for a way to train people more rapidly into our culture. We therefore engaged Dr. Joe Kavanaugh, a professor of business strategy at Sam Houston State University, to perform a project to better define the culture.

We proceeded by proposing one hundred questions that we would ask our employees about Stress and its culture. Some questions were worded in such a way that a positive response was good, and some were worded in the negative. All employees—well, over four hundred at the time—were asked to answer all the questions. When they did, the responses were tabulated by location. By then, we had three locations in Houston, New Orleans, and Cincinnati.

Dr. Kavanaugh engaged another professor, Dr. Mehta, to perform a statistical analysis of the answers and determine which questions were answered similar enough to hang together. We found that eleven groups of the questions did hang together. We then assembled a team of senior leaders at Stress and Dr. Kavanaugh to determine what the statements collectively meant. This process resulted in the "Eleven Elements of Stress Culture" shown here:

Eleven Elements of Stress Culture©

1. We accept and solve clients' hard problems and that requires continuous development of expertise.
2. What is valued is clear and rewarded. Employees are highly valued. What everyone has to do to succeed is clear.
3. We work hard to deliver the right stuff on time. This leads to repeat business and success.
4. Employees are hired because of ability. We succeed because of teamwork.
5. Our service areas must align with customers' needs and emerging markets.
6. Repeated professional performance is appreciated and rewarded.
7. Employees are trusted to perform their responsibilities. This permits self-direction.
8. We have minimal top-down management.
9. We're all in the same boat and expected to share the same essential professional and organizational goals.
10. Personal responsibility—It is a serious violation of the standards of Stress to put a colleague or the organization at risk of failure and is likely to carry serious consequences.
11. Risk is to be managed in professional work and business decisions.

Copyright Stress Engineering Services Inc. Used with permission.

The resulting elements are interesting and much richer than the four items I had taught for a long time. There is no doubt that the four are encompassed in all the items, but some were complete surprises. The most surprising to me was number 7: Employees are trusted to perform their responsibilities. This permits self-direction.

Before then, I did not realize how important it is to employees to feel trusted. As I talked to a number of individuals who had worked at other companies, they said that being trusted is *not* the norm at most companies. The other side of item 7 are items 10 and 11—it is every employee's personal responsibility to not put the company or another employee at risk of failure, and the fact that risk has to be managed in professional work and business decisions.

I would advise anyone starting a company to consider these items in developing personnel, training, customer service, and business management policies. Particularly consider the tension between item 7 (trust employees) and items 10 and 11 (personal responsibility and risk management). In setting procedures for work review, quality assurance, contract review, and personnel policies, consider not only protecting the company but also how the policies relate to employees in regard to trusting them.

Upon completing the analysis of Stress's culture and based on the eleven elements that emerged from the study, Dr. Kavanaugh's research proposed the following clear interpretive narrative:

> Continuous development of expertise as engineers, professionals, and as a firm is paramount. That is how we build our business. This is accomplished by working new problems, accepting challenging work, and applying a diversity of talent in teams that produce higher-quality solutions. Goal-directed performance that develops expertise and builds the business is rewarded. It is management's responsibility to provide the necessary resources and a supportive work environment that encourages autonomy and fosters an ownership ethic while providing equitable rewards based on performance. It is a serious violation of the standards of Stress to put a colleague or the organization at risk of failure and is likely to carry serious consequences. Risk is to be managed in professional work and business decisions.
>
> — Kavanaugh and Mehta, used with permission

Employee Review and Evaluation System

Historically, most companies appreciate the importance of employee review and evaluation, but the implementation often does more harm than good. At Stress, we wanted the process to result in continuous improvement of employees, so we devised a system that was difficult to implement but gave very good feedback to employees.

Typically, companies will devise a review system that depends upon some objective measure of the employee's work and the opinion of the boss (immediate supervisor) of that person. In a company that has a simple organization with not too much interaction between work groups, that may be fine. But in a consulting organization that requires cooperation among widely different groups in different locations and many people in the company, it won't work very well because the boss can't see all the interactions between different employee groups and really has no good way to evaluate the effectiveness of the employee in those interactions.

In our peer review system, everyone had the opportunity to evaluate everyone else. This is called a 360-degree system since employees could evaluate anyone, including the president (me). When you consider that we performed more than 2,500 projects a year for eight hundred clients annually and had almost five hundred employees, that most projects utilized two or more practices with different leaders and that most projects utilized two to fifteen people, you realize that this is the only way to get a true picture of how each employee is really doing.

We started this practice in the 1980s, at a time that the staff was small enough that the data could be reduced and compiled with the help of a spreadsheet program. Later, we used software from several vendors. The evaluations were in a numerical form with answers to a few simple questions like competence, cooperation, and productivity of the employee being evaluated with an opportunity for a comment about the employee. The evaluation each employee received was in the form of a numerical average for each question and a compilation of the comments. The comments were anonymous unless the rater wanted to sign them.

There were two levels of review to the process. First, I edited each comment to eliminate hurtful or nonconstructive comments. There were often several thousand comments; the substance of them was not changed, but they were sometimes reworded to be constructive. Second, each employee's supervisor reviewed the complete evaluation before it was given to the employee. Prior to starting the process, we held a training session to instruct everyone about rating only those people with whom you had worked during the year and not submitting destructive comments. Examples were given of how to do this.

The process worked well for more than thirty years, and I think it worked because of our good culture and because employees perceived it was administered fairly. It gave current, accurate information about the perception of the performance of each employee from everyone, whether above or below the person being rated, who had had an opportunity to observe that person's behavior.

Employees really care what their peers think of them. If there is an area that needs improvement, it is far more likely that the employee will believe it's the truth if the feedback comes from fellow workers rather than just the boss's opinion. If the boss reinforces the observations of coworkers about areas that need improvement, it is very likely the employee will actually work hard to improve in that area.

In addition to peer reviews, evaluation included other data like annual hours charged to clients for professional engineers and technicians, quality of project management, and success of work in other administrative functions like accounting, administration, marketing, maintenance, etc.

Satellite Offices

We started the Cincinnati office in 1992 at a major customer's request. This office has grown over the years and remains a major strength of Stress. Most of the work is consumer product and medical and other product development, but the office also services many clients in the Midwest with traditional industrial services.

In 1996, we started the New Orleans office with Greg Garic and Glenn Aucoin as leaders. It was designed to offer traditional Stress services to the upstream, downstream, and midstream energy industry. The realization there was that the clients really appreciated a local company, and the area is home to the second largest collection of these firms in the country. For a few years, we also operated a Baton Rouge office out of the New Orleans office.

In 1999, we acquired the Mohr engineering and testing operation and operated it as a separate office. We started a new subsea engineering practice in 2003 under Kerry Kirkland. In 2012, we acquired the practice of Robert Thom in Calgary, Canada, and started Stress Engineering Canada. We already did a lot of projects in Canada, and combining practices allowed us to better serve Canadian customers and dramatically grow the business.

In 2013, we started Stress Engineering and Construction under Dave Masterson in Houston to provide engineering, procurement, and construction management services (EPC) to the refinery and chemical plant sectors. Also, over the years, we operated offices in Atlanta and Denver that were closed when they were not successful because of market changes and the lack of a diverse local group of clients.

The challenges of a new operation were primarily getting the culture of Stress implanted and developing a critical mass of customers and staff. All these operations have always been run financially out of Stress Houston as far as billing, payroll, accounts receivable and accounts payable, and contracts. But the leaders of each office were responsible for the business of securing and servicing clients and managing the employees located there.

It takes a lot of combined effort on the part of Houston management and the local management to make this work. Overall, the concept of distributed offices for a professional service firm is really necessary to enjoy a national practice and to be of real service to national and international clients.

Importance of All Staff Members

At Stress, we were blessed with some great support staff over the years. First, for many years, Teri Shackelford was responsible for accounting and contracts as well as being a project support person. She had a wonderful can-do attitude. As the company grew, we were lucky to get Helen Chan, CPA, to become our chief accountant in 1993. She supervised our finances as the company grew to almost five hundred employees. She brought a great professionalism to the business, and our policies of always paying early or on time resulted in a lot of dedicated vendors.

Linda Kenney did our human resources work, and today, Stress has an outstanding HR staff headed by Donya Brewer. Our first full-time lawyer, Angela Dunlap, who was hired as the contracting process became more in-depth and complicated (especially after the BP Macondo blowout, spill, and fire in 2010), has done a great job of growing with the company and keeping Stress out of the courthouse. The magnitude and scope of Macondo caused everyone in the offshore industry to look carefully at their contracts.

Our first safety person was Dr. Ed Bailey, who did that work as an extra duty to his busy consulting practice because of his true dedication to safety. Danny Krzywicki, who was hired after we had a serious accident in one of our labs in 1999, has done a great job of keeping our people safe by really teaching everyone how to work safely and how to keep safety uppermost in everyone's mind. Safety has become the most important objective of the company, and Danny is the consummate professional. Earl Hudspeth was our first professional quality assurance person who organized our work to ensure it is correct. Judy Osmon has been our lead receptionist for many years who knows most of the clients, and most of them greet her with a hug. Delilah Rodriguez helped me personally with organization and documents and was my right-hand assistant with a great attitude. As Ron Young said, "If you were in a foxhole, you would want Delilah with you."

Stress has an outstanding IT staff led by Matt Mistric, who started with the company as a teenager before college. Stress has been blessed with a lot of top-notch administrative and technician staff in addition to the core engineers.

Ownership Transition Strategy

In the end, every business is sold or goes out of business from the perspective of the founder. No one lives forever. Most entrepreneurial businesses are designed to be sold to an acquirer or to the public if the business goes public. Stress was developed and run as a professional practice with many shareholders who were sold shares after the individual professional developed to the point they were significant to the business.

When the business is small, this works well; but as the company develops substantially, it becomes too valuable for incoming shareholders to purchase without help. We studied different solutions to this conundrum and felt that selling the business to an outside firm would not be good for the employees. As we had observed for a long time, when a business is sold, the new owner puts in their management. Usually, the new management's job is to get a financial return on the money the new owner paid for the business. This is frequently done by limiting payments for salaries and bonuses to employees, which leads to the good employees leaving. Typically, it takes about five years for the company to disappear.

The senior owners—Tom Asbill, Ron Young, and I—did not want that to happen. In 2005, we proposed an employee stock ownership plan (ESOP) that would result in the company being owned by the ESOP. ESOPs had been around for more than twenty-five years. Basically, the plan is 100 percent funded by the company, and it is actually a tax-deferred employee benefit program. If the company is an S corporation (as Stress had been for many years), no corporate taxes are paid each year on the share of company income owned by the ESOP. The employees' distributions after retirement are taxable like a 401(k).

So we started an ESOP in 2005 and began funding it with company contributions. Actually, we simply changed the 10 percent of the bonus plan we had been making as company contributions to the 401(k) to the ESOP instead. Everyone who was not already an owner was very glad to get a piece of the rock. The company contributes money to the ESOP, and the ESOP buys retiring shareholders' shares as they retire. The stock is then recycled to employees as a benefit similar to the company contribution to the 401(k).

By the end of 2014, the ESOP was worth more than $64 million. In 2015, we had an unsolicited offer to purchase the company for the market value. The principals (shareholders with a prescribed ownership level, about thirty people) considered the offer (Ron

Young and I did not vote; we planned to retire in the next couple of years, and sadly, Tom Asbill had passed away in 2011) but decided not to accept it.

An ESOP is a worthy choice for an ownership transition strategy in a services business where revenue is relatively steady. There are more than ten thousand ESOP companies in the USA, and many analyses have shown that ESOP companies are more profitable and more stable than non-ESOP companies.

Pay Practices and Financial Results

From the start, the strategy of Stress was to pay employees competitive (but never excessive) base pay, with the opportunity for employees to make more through overtimes and bonuses. Most companies did not—and still don't—pay overtime to professionals, so this is significant since our average engineer worked overtime for twenty hours a month. In addition, our bonus program paid 40 percent of the cash profits to the employees and 10 percent as contributions to the ESOP. Most nonprincipal employees would receive about 12.5 percent of their base annual salary as a bonus.

Growth Rates, 1983–2014

Sales, profits, and number of employees compounded at 15.5 percent, 19.7 percent, and 9.2 percent, respectively, compounded annual growth rate for the thirty-two years I was president. This is due to great partners, great spouses, and great employees serving industries that really needed our help and lots of help from the Man Upstairs.

After I retired, the principals selected Jack Miller as president; and he continues to do an outstanding job with the help of Randy Long, Chuck Miller, Clint Haynes, and Terry Lechinger.

•

Stress Engineering Services Inc., c. 2015.

Crafting Stress Engineering Services Inc.

Tom Asbill, Joe Fowler, Ron Young, c. 2005.

Ed Bailey, c. 2005.

Six

Stress Engineering Services Inc. and Industry History

Some historical events had dramatic effects on Stress Engineering Services Inc. A list of the more significant ones follows. Some happened before Stress was born in 1972, but each had an impact.

- 1859. Edwin Drake's discovery well in Pennsylvania made possible the first US refinery that made kerosene in 1862. Kerosene replaced whale oil for lighting.
- 1863. Standard Oil Trust, now Exxon, was formed.
- 1901. Spindletop ushered in the modern production industry with a one-hundred-thousand-barrel-per-day discovery near Beaumont, Texas.
- 1907. The merger of Royal Dutch Shell.
- 1908. Model T—there were 125,000 automobiles in US.
- 1909. British Petroleum (BP) was formed.
- 1911. Standard Oil was broken up by US government. Exxon, Mobil, Chevron, Sohio, Amoco, and Atlantic Richfield became separate entities.
- 1913. Thermal cracking is the start of modern refineries by chemically altering the hydrocarbon molecules rather than refining crude by separating by density through distillation.
- 1939–1946. US refineries made 80 percent of fuel used by Allies during World War II.

- 1942. U-boats sank seventy-four ships. New pipelines, Big Inch (twenty-four-inch diameter) and Little Inch (twenty-inch diameter), were built from Texas to East Coast to ship crude and refined products. This year was the start of our big pipeline industry.
- 1954. First jack-up rig was built for Zapata (owned by George H. W. Bush) by Letourneau.
- 1969. Santa Barbara oil spill spilled eighty thousand to one hundred thousand barrels; Offshore Technology Conference (OTC) was formed.
- 1970. EPA was established; US production peaked.
- 1972. Stress Engineering Services Inc. was founded.
- 1973–74. Marine riser work started at Stress.
- 1979. Three Mile Island nuclear accident in Pennsylvania stopped construction of nuclear plants in US.
- 1980. Alexander Kielland submersible rig capsized in the North Sea due to a fatigue failure and killed 123 people.
- 1981–1989. Depression in oil patch because of low petroleum prices.
- 1984. Conoco tension-leg well platform was first launched in the Gulf of Mexico. Stress designed the drilling rig and well system.
- 1985. Chevron bought Gulf Oil.
- 1989. Piper Alpha was destroyed in explosion and fire in the North Sea, killing 167 men and shutting down 10 percent of the North Sea production.
- 1989. Exxon Valdez ran aground in Alaska, spilling 260,000 to nine hundred thousand barrels of oil.
- 1998. BP acquired Amoco.
- 1999. Stress bought Mohr Research & Engineering.
- 2001. Chevron bought Texaco.
- 2001. World Trade Center terrorist attack on US happened.
- 2005. BP Texas City Refinery disaster killed fifteen; Stress ESOP was formed.
- 2010. Deepwater Horizon sank; it killed eleven men and discharged 4.9 million barrels of oil into the Gulf of Mexico from the BP Macondo well.
- 2016-2017. Depression in oil patch from low petroleum prices.

Of these events, many were significant to Stress. The 1954 jack-up rig paved the way for floating units and the need for marine risers, which became a large service area. The Santa Barbara oil spill in 1969 was the basis for my PhD work on floating oil containment barriers and introduction to the engineering methods of calculating the effects on pipes and structures from waves and currents in the ocean.

The 1979 Three Mile Island accident essentially stopped our work on certified stress reports for nuclear power plants. The Alexander Kielland and Piper Alpha North Sea accidents made crystal clear to the world that the risks of offshore operations were real, and serious operators needed to pay attention to the details of their work. Stress was, and still is, one of the few independent engineering companies offering to provide the services operators really needed, and that made for good business for Stress.

After the World Trade Center attack in 2001, our insurance underwriters did not want to even quote rates for our business since their capacity had been so impaired. With the help of our insurance agent, Allen Wilson, we made a video that described the safety, quality assurance, contract review, and attitudes that we had that resulted in our record of zero claims. We got reasonable rates after that. The underwriters had to dig into the details of our work to understand that we were safe, and our video made that easy for them during a stressful time.

The BP Texas City disaster in 2005 brought the same awareness to the need for our services in the refineries, and a number of very serious pipeline failures did the same thing for our pipeline engineering business. The Deepwater Horizon accident reminded all the need for careful, accurate engineering and testing in deepwater drilling and led to a huge increase in demand for our services.

Companies have to be adaptive and willing to meet the changes that will inevitably occur in the marketplace as we at Stress have had to do continually in our history. There truly is nothing constant but change.

•

Seven

The Importance of Goal Setting

As an entrepreneur who thoroughly enjoyed starting businesses, I really did not focus on the science of managing them until the late 1980s and early 1990s. Our attitude at Stress had been to continually hunt for business and opportunities that provided adequate margins, and the company grew steadily using our basic business model of providing niche services to company clients who needed help. That worked well for a smaller company, but by 1986 (when I was forty), Stress had only about twenty to thirty employees. The Strawberry Tub, for sure, had more than that.

Then my dad died in 1987, and I realized I needed to change how I operated. I quit smoking, started running, lost weight, and began to seriously think about the development of our business and me personally. First, I worked very hard; and by 1990, I had developed a personal mission statement that has changed some over the years but is still essentially the same with a focus on God, family, businesses in which I am involved, and giving back to those in need.

Then I started developing goals and objectives for me, for our family, and for Stress. This focus on goals and objectives helped to really accelerate the growth of Stress. Within a few years, the business leaders of Stress were involved in this, and we had planning sessions for each practice area and the overall company. These were annually presented to all the shareholders in detail and to all employees at a high level.

The Importance of Goal Setting

What was—and still is—amazing to me is how these goals and objectives we laid out for the most part came true!

Science of Goal Setting

Although I actually was not aware of the reasons it worked when I started goal setting, there is a real rational basis for its success in improving the performance of individuals and organizations, and there is real science behind the need to set goals.

Setting goals increases motivation. If you are reminded periodically of your objectives, they are more likely to get done. Many studies show that having goals also increases achievement. In the engineering world, President John Kennedy's announcement in 1961 to put a man on the moon in that decade spurred a whole industry to actually achieve that on July 20, 1969, when Neil Armstrong stepped onto the moon's surface.

SMART Goals

Lots of engineers are taught to make goals SMART: specific, measureable, attainable, realistic, and time bound. This works for everyone, not just engineers.

In my case, for Stress, the goals were annual, along the following lines:

1. Achieve sales of X with profit margins of Y.
2. Improve the culture in a specific practice.
3. Get an office started in Z.
4. Start a new practice area in W.
5. Improve the performance of Mr. V.

I referred to them often. Goals 1, 3, and 4 are very easy to evaluate at the end of the year. Goals 2 and 5 are subjective goals, but at the end of a period, you know if you are actually making progress.

I also maintain(ed) family and personal goals. These were like the following:

1. Help a family member to achieve a specific goal or improve a problem area in their life.
2. Achieve a financial goal, like paying off a mortgage or saving a given amount of money for retirement or children's college.
3. Improve my health by specific habits of diet and exercise.
4. Achieve some other family goal.

In my mind, these are like a daily to-do list but on a much longer timescale. As I evaluate these periodically or at the end of a year, I either eliminate them if they have been achieved or are no longer needed or propose a change for the next year if conditions have changed or results were not satisfactory.

What is really amazing after a number of years is that this process really works!

●

EIGHT

Technologies of Tomorrow

In the earlier section "Back in the Day," I told of the technologies used when I started practicing engineering—slide rules, hand plotting and drawing, and slow mainframe computers. Today, technology advances at a breakneck pace in all areas. According to the news, futurists, and researchers, the technologies of tomorrow have the promise to dramatically improve lives for everyone. Currently, I serve on the Board of Governors of the American Society of Mechanical Engineers (ASME), which has identified five key technologies we believe are going to be crucial to the future. They are bioengineering, robotics, pressure technology, manufacturing, and clean energy. ASME aims to be a leader among the professional societies in these five. Furthermore, I believe tomorrow's technologies will advance in particular ways.

First, biomedical devices and technology will include the science of genetics and DNA, and they already do. We know that many diseases and afflictions are at least partially caused by genetics. Also, the future of individual medical treatment based partially on genetics is upon us now.

Continually improved computers and the software (apps) that drive them will be developed and applied in all areas of technology. Moore's law, proposed in 1965 by Gordon Moore (an Intel founder), states that the number of transistors that can be placed on a circuit doubles every two years. This means double the computer power at far less than double the cost. Few industries have seen such real productivity improvement as computers, although the process improvements of computers applied to many industries has those industries far more efficient.

Moore's prediction has actually been conservative, although there is speculation that the computing power will stop increasing quite so fast. In any event, there will come a day—and many predict in not too many years—when computers with advanced artificial intelligence software will rival the intelligence of humans. What then? This is a huge area for mankind.

Next, power from renewable resources of wind, solar, and biomass will dramatically increase. This will happen as the cost of renewable power decreases, relative to power from nonrenewable sources. The income per person of a country, or the world, is proportional to the energy use per person, and many projections have the world population growing from 7.6 billion people in 2018 to over nine billion in 2040. More energy per capita equals more income per capita. Thus, for real standards of living to increase, it is likely that energy use overall will increase substantially. Also, there are fears that more carbon dioxide being generated by energy production from oil, gas, and coal will cause the earth to become significantly hotter. These trends push the world toward the use of much more renewable energy like solar and wind. Most of the good locations to make hydroelectric power are already being used for that.

Today, major problems with wind and solar are that they are often not available when and where they are needed. For example, Texas has the largest installed base of wind power of any state in the nation, but the record for generating wind power occurred on a night in the fall when electricity needs were minimal. Inexpensive storage will be key to enabling the technology necessary for the advancement of wind and solar energy. Materials and nanotechnology will likely be the key to solving this challenge.

Robotics will be a huge technology of the future. It already is today. Most folks have seen the pictures of robots building cars in Toyota factories. They are awesome! Robotics will be a key in enabling technology for many industries. Robots will be used to inspect places like the inside of pressure vessels and pipes where people can't go, to inspect structures and building from above (drones), in self-driving cars that are really robots, and countless other examples where the work that needs to be done can be done cheaper and safer by robots.

Three-dimensional printers can print parts made of many materials, including steel. Today, parts come from the mind of a designer, to a digital math model on a computer, and to a finished part printed by a 3-D printer. This is advanced manufacturing.

Supersonic (above the speed of sound) aircraft was outlawed for private use in 1972 to avoid disturbing cities with the noise from sonic booms. Today, advanced engineering and materials bring forth the possibility that aircraft with supersonic capability can be developed and fly without sonic booms. This will greatly reduce travel time to faraway destinations overseas and to other parts of the country, while having the potential to bring the world's people closer together.

Interplanetary travel is a goal of many people. Rockets made by private companies are greatly reducing the cost of space travel. And for the first time in many years, our government is starting to consider encouraging and funding this activity and has recently selected the next class of astronauts, again, the first in many years.

Concerns

One of the first concerns about technology is about jobs. Will robots be able to do work so cheaply that humans can't compete? This has been a fear since the Industrial Revolution began.

What has happened, of course, is that the work has changed. In 1870, most workers were busy in the growing of food and fiber for human subsistence. By 2008, less than 2 percent of workers were so engaged. The jobs of the future will require people to be educated in the technologies that drive the economy. But the wonder of the United States from its beginning is that the individual freedoms we enjoy enable each person to structure their career to take advantage of what the economy needs.

Who would have thought in 1900 that in 2018, there would be $33 billion spent on pizza, over four million people working in the fast-food industry, or seven hundred thousand people working in the nail care industry? Or who could have predicted in 1960 that by 2018 (this writing), smartphones would have totally changed how we work and interact with one another? Or that there would be almost four million computer programmers in the US and almost twenty-six million worldwide?

Many people are employed writing apps for these devices that combine phones, computers, cameras, calendars, and numerous other functions; and essentially, all adults carry one with them continually. The jobs will change and have continued to constantly change. Young people need to be educated in the basic sciences behind these technologies and the principles that control them. Young people also need a strong moral upbringing and to be taught how to *think*. The huge advantage that the US has over all other large countries is the individual freedom that citizens enjoy. Individuals are free to pursue their dream of building the business of their dreams. This is unlike most other countries where government control of all programs and businesses makes it very hard to start a new business, and there is no culture of doing so.

From the founding of our country, Americans have had to mostly do it themselves to be successful in their lives, and the result is the country with the highest productive output in the world. The US gross national product (GDP) is over 60 percent higher than number 2 China, which has 1.4 billion people versus the US with 330 million.

Another fear is that the movie *Terminator* will somehow come true with robots smarter, stronger, and faster than humans to displace us as the dominant species on earth. Just as it is the responsibility of our federal government to protect us from other people who want to harm us, it will be our own responsibility, working through our governments, to prevent this. Someday there may be a police force whose job is to detect and stop "terminators," or bad artificial people. If history has taught us anything, it is that mankind is capable of hatred, genocide, thievery, and murder. We must be vigilant to instill strong ethics and values in our children and remain strong as a society.

Yet another fear is that longer life spans will cause most people to outlive their assets and result in one of our most basic fears—that of poverty in old age. Again, this is both a personal and societal responsibility. Individuals should plan for their own old age, families should take care of their own older members, and our governments should provide a basic level of care for those unfortunate elderly folks who have neither family nor assets.

A related fear is the opposite. If new medical or genetic breakthroughs result in people being able to have an essentially infinite lifespan, who decides who gets to experience this if there are not enough resources for all? Perhaps we should pray about this one.

New technologies inevitably will result in many ethical and societal dilemmas. For sure, we will still need churches, laws, lawyers, justice systems, and armies to deal with them.

•

NINE

Hindsight's Perspective: Tips for Success and Giving Back

By three methods we may learn wisdom: First by reflection, which is noblest; second by imitation, which is easiest; and third by experience, which is the bitterest.

—Confucius

Tip 1
Really get good at your craft. Learn the work very well. If you have great skills, you can really help your company. Never stop learning!

We hired a recent PhD graduate in mechanical engineering from a noted Texas private university. He had studied under a famous professor in drilling mechanics, so we thought he would do well. After a number of months, our project managers didn't want to use him. I didn't want to give up on him, so I got him to help me on a little project I had. The client wanted to know what would happen if they dropped a four-hundred-thousand-pound blowout preventer (BOP) in five thousand feet of water in a two-knot (3.38 feet per second) current. How far from the drop point might it drift? They were planning for such an event and needed to know how large to build their ocean floor protection for their equipment.

So I showed him the equations to use to calculate horizontal and vertical fluid forces on the BOP as it fell and suggested he write a simple program to do the calculations. He came back in ten days or so and had the answer that the watch circle (how far it might drift in any direction) was about one-half inch, and it took the stack about two to three minutes to fall five thousand feet.

"Really?" I said. That answer could not be correct. At that fall, velocity-to-upward-drag forces are many times the weight, and the watch circle did not make physical sense. I asked him to redo the work, and he came back in a day or two with reasonable answers.

"What was wrong?" I asked.

And he sheepishly answered, "Units problem."

Freshman engineering students are all routinely drilled on proper units conversion. They also are taught to check their results for reasonableness. Needless to say, I had to discharge him.

Businesspersons today are in for a world of constant change. No one will prepare you for this but yourself. You must continually develop personal technical skills and be willing to expand your horizons throughout your career. You will be at a serious disadvantage in the competitive workplace otherwise. Plan on attending at least one short course a year; participate in ongoing professional development, including some type of self-study project if possible; and go to professional societies—for engineers, those like the American Society of Mechanical Engineers (ASME).

No one except you can—or should—take responsibility for the potential ramifications of the wrenching changes that are very likely to continue as part of our business climate. You must prepare as best you can through continued educational development and a wide circle of contacts and friends. Of course, this is the invigorating way to participate in a volatile economy and certainly the most interesting way to meet the challenge.

Advanced formal education is very important if you can at all afford it. As long ago as 1990, the average MS engineer made $6,600 per year more than the BS, and the average PhD made $17,000 more than the BS. More importantly, the engineers with advanced training, whether in engineering, business, or law, have far more career advancement potential than those without.

As a point of reference, the recent CEO of a Houston technical firm held both BS and MS degrees in electrical engineering from the University of Houston. The CEO of General Electric held a PhD from the University of Illinois. The CEO of the largest pharmaceutical firm in the US was an MD. The heads of most of the major oil companies are people with technical undergraduate degrees and graduate degrees in law, business, or engineering. The message is clear. An advanced degree is an important advantage in comparing your capability to others and in your desirability to employers.

Money, of course, is far from everything. Integrity as a fundamental personal quality is more important than ever. Lawsuits happen for two reasons. First, there is the economic incentive for the plaintiff's attorney, who typically gets 40 percent of any judgment; and second, someone usually did not act with complete integrity. If you treat your fellow employees, your employer, your customers, and your suppliers with integrity, you are much less likely to be sued; and you will also be much more successful long-term.

Tip 2
Learn the concept of completed staff work. When you are given a job to do, do it! Get help if you need it; don't flounder if you are stuck. Ask for help, but finish the job!

I attended a course by Larry Steinmetz, former professor at the Graduate School of Business at the University of Colorado. His lifetime research was why companies and organizations buy from particular vendors. Surprisingly, it is not price, it is not personal relationships, and it is not quality although each of those is a factor. The overriding factor overall is the right stuff on time.

All companies who buy products and services from vendors do so to keep their own operations running smoothly. Whether the purchaser is a manufacturing company, a utility, a retailer, or a service company, they need the vendor's product to keep their operation running smoothly.

If the vendor's product is wrong, it doesn't help them. If the vendor's product is late, it doesn't help them. Only the correct product or service on time helps the customer, and the vendor who can deliver the right stuff on time will have plenty of business.

Tip 3
Have a good attitude and show respect. Be a good team member. Ignorance and arrogance together are especially dangerous.

Hindsight's Perspective: Tips for Success and Giving Back

To succeed in a company, work on the project or product that is most important to the success of the company. Don't allow yourself to be placed on some product that is not significant. It will hurt your ultimate advancement and make you vulnerable to layoffs in hard times.

To succeed in a company, people skills are as important (some would say more important) than any other skills. You should develop positive relationships with people at all levels in the company and not ignore the social side of your job. You may say this is politics, but the world is run by people, and their feelings and sensitivities often motivate their actions, especially when making personnel decisions. Your relationships, however, must be genuine; as my experience is that phonies are rarely successful long-term. Maintain friendships with colleagues in other companies and other industries as well. These can be beneficial to you both. ASME or other societies or organizations are a great place to make these sorts of friendships based on technical fellowship.

To succeed, you should learn at least a modicum of business skills. Accounting is the language of business, and if you cannot read and understand a financial statement, you will be at a long-term disadvantage. Any community college can provide this training. You also should learn a foreign language. This is hard, and I wish someone had made me do it twenty to thirty years ago. Another language will be an enormous and continuing advantage, particularly in today's ever-expanding world.

Tip 4
Care about your team members personally (all levels). This will make or break your career.

All the human resources literature shows, and my own experience is that the number one reason people leave jobs is that they don't get along with their boss. And the corollary is that good bosses know that if they remove a person causing bad morale, the work productivity of a work group always improves dramatically. I have seen these HR lessons time and time again.

In the main, change is constant and inevitable, and advanced higher education is generally a great investment. You must take responsibility for your own career and professional development, and knowledge in business and foreign cultures will be increasingly important.

Tip 5
Recognize the importance of giving back to the community—and ways to do it.

In "Charting a Course," I talked about my opinion that it is important to follow John Wesley's advice to make all you can, save all you can, and give all you can. But how do you do that with your business? Where should you give it?

First, consider the nature of the various not-for-profits. Their natures are quite different. The churches' mission is to bring people closer to God, and certainly everyone who is a believer in the Almighty God should support the church of their choice. If someone is a sole owner of a business, they can give company money to a church, and that is technically their business. But consider the nature of our employee groups in America. At Stress, we had Christians of many denominations, Muslims, Buddhists, Sikhs, and others. If a sole owner gives significant company resources to a particular church, this will eventually become known and may be a wedge between employees and the owner. If a multiple-owner firm gives large amounts of company money directly to a church, and the owners are not all aligned among themselves as to which is the preferred church, that will become a point of division between them and is also bad for the company. So in my opinion, church contributions are best made by individual owners out of the money paid by the company to the owners in the form of salary, bonuses, or dividends. Religious beliefs are so personal that is it best not to get them mixed up with the company. In America, in order to have successful companies, we need employees selected based on their ability and attitudes and work ethic and not religious beliefs.

Second, consider broad-based charities unaffiliated with the industry such as United Way, the Salvation Army, American Heart Association, the American Cancer Society, and local charities like Northwest Assistance Ministries and REACH in Houston and others that serve needs of the local community. Company money given to these charities serves the local needy, and all employees can get behind and support these groups. Over the years, Stress and the Strawberry Tub and Linda and I personally supported all these. At Stress, our United Way campaigns were to encourage employees to give out of their money, with company money being primarily used for employee time to run the campaign plus some money for prizes.

Third, consider the nonprofit associations and societies, which are professional societies, like the American Society of Mechanical Engineers (ASME), the American Society of Civil Engineers (ASCE), the American Institute of Chemical Engineers (AIChe), the Society of Petroleum Engineers (SPE), and many others. These provide valuable services to our employee members, including training and certification, and also do separate charitable programs like scholarships.

At Stress, we supported, with company funds, those we felt were worthy and helped promote the mission of our company. We also paid the dues for employees who were society members and encouraged them to volunteer to help promote their mission and provided some work time to employees to carry out the volunteer work. Also, the societies help our employees remain at the top of their game with the training provided and also network with clients and potential clients. Overall, this is an excellent use of company resources.

Over my career, I spent a lot of time (company and my personal time) doing ASME work, including important national offices. Currently, I serve on the Board of Governors of ASME. Previously, I was president of ABET, which accredits all the engineering programs in the US, and was board chair of the Offshore Technology Conference, which is the offshore industry's largest event with fifty to one hundred thousand attendees.

Fourth, consider the trade associations like the American Petroleum Institute (API), which is also a standards organization. Others in the petroleum industry are the Petroleum Equipment Suppliers Association (PESA) and the National Ocean Industries Association (NOIA). These are also excellent potential uses of company funds as they provide networking, training, standards, and other functions that are often very helpful to the company. Supporting them with funds and employee time is another excellent use of company resources. The industry meets together at their meetings; we get to work with clients as coworkers to help make the industry better for everyone.

Fifth, consider the universities that educate our employees and have multiple fundraising arms raising funds for good causes, like scholarships and research. Generally, these are not good places for company funds because of the strong affinity employees have for their university. Linda and I have personally given large amounts of our personal money to fund scholarships and other programs at Texas A&M University, and we take a lot of personal pride in helping educate many dozens of young folks over the years. We believe in the educational mission and the value of the training the young folks receive, *but* all the donations have been personal money and not company money. Other Stress principals have allegiance to other fine schools, and it would be not be right for the company to support one school over another.

Money is not the only resource companies have to share. The time of employees, particularly executives, is crucial to the success of the organizations and is more important than money.

Finally, many executives and employees have a personal passion for a particular charity because the employee believes the work is important and supports it with their own money. Linda and I have been strong supporters of NAM, the Pearl Fincher Museum of Fine Arts, and the Impact Church of Christ Brooks Scholarship Program for underprivileged young adults. This program has provided a college scholarship to many dozens of young people that has resulted in changing the trajectory of their family. All these are good and follow the John Wesley principle.

I believe we are not alone in wanting to leave the world and society a better place than we found it, and I think most entrepreneurs would agree.

•

Ten

Granddaddy's Investing Advice

This is for new or novice investors to help them get started in investing. It is a collection of questions from a new investor's viewpoint and from my own experience.

First, why invest at all? Why not just spend my money as I get it?

Investing is for the future to make it easier for yourself or someone you love. The idea is to put money away and hopefully watch it grow until it is needed (by you or someone you love). Assets will make it possible to do things you couldn't do otherwise, like go to college, buy a house, start a business, retire comfortably, help a charity, or pursue your dream.

What is the magic of compounding, and why does it matter so much?

When you invest money, you hope to make a return on the money—that is, to earn money on the money itself. If you invest that return rather than spending it, then the return can earn money also. If that is reinvested, it earns money too. It can grow like magic!

All investors need to learn the rule of 72, which is math you can do in your head. Take the number of years you have an investment times the return per year in percent. When the two equal 72, your money has doubled. For example, at 6 percent interest, your money doubles in twelve years. At 2 percent interest, it takes thirty-six years!

The US stock market has returned an *average* of around 10 percent annually for over ninety years. If you compound money for fifty years (very possible for young beginning investors), then fifty years times 10 percent equals 500. Divide by 72, and that is almost seven doubles. A dollar that doubles seven times is $128 after fifty years! If you got only 5 percent interest for fifty years, then 50 times five equals 250. Divide by 72, and that is about three-and-one-half doubles. So one dollar would turn into about $11.30. Do the math and check me!

That's quite a difference. So working on getting the highest return is important in investing. And we will talk about *risk* a little later because there really is no free lunch in investing.

What are the main differences between investments?

Investments are basically ownership of an asset or loans to a business, government, or individual. The owners of businesses use loans because they think they can make more money by paying interest to the lenders (people who lend the money) than by paying partners a share of the profits. As a business owner, I can borrow money to pay for equipment in my business or sell a part of my business as stock in the business to raise the money. With the lender, I just have to pay back the loan. But I have to pay the partner their share of the profits forever (or until I buy back their stock)!

When you own stock in a business, you assume the financial risk or reward of how the business does. When you lend money, you get your money back and a small, defined return and no more. As mentioned above, stocks in businesses have returned 10 percent on average for ninety years. Today, banks are making loans for around 5 percent. So considering the magic of compounding, long-term stocks have been far better investments.

There are many other types of investments. Among the most important is real estate, which represents the fundamental value of property. It has been a great investment in the right locations with properties that both pay rent from tenants and appreciate in value.

What are the risks of various investments?

Stocks have two main risks. The first is that the company does bad and goes out of business. Unlike Apple and Google, there are a lot of start-up companies that are not successful and lose all their owners' money. But large companies are safer, and a group of ten to twenty large companies is safer still. A mutual fund is an investment that owns many stocks. And a large mutual fund that owns stock in thousands of companies has very little risk of an individual company failing.

The second risk is that the market as a whole will go down, which it regularly does. This usually ties to a decline in the overall economy like what happened in 2008–2009. The Depression in the 1930s resulted in the stock market being down for many years. Investors have to understand this and be prepared for periods when their investments lose money. Still, over very long periods, the average return on stocks has been about 10 percent.

Small companies grow faster than big companies. And small company returns generally have been more than 2 percent a year greater than large companies, but they are more volatile.

Given that stocks can go down, how should you divide your money among investment types?

From the ancient Jewish text the Talmud, a record of debates among rabbis about Jewish law, dating as early as 1200 BCE, comes this advice: "Let every man divide his money into three parts, and invest a third in land, a third in business, and a third let him keep by him in reserve." So people have worried about this for a very long time. A modern-day translation of this might be a third in stocks, a third in real estate, and a third in bonds.

If you want to improve your investment results, I suggest two books: *The Intelligent Asset Allocator* by William Bernstein and *Asset Allocation: Balancing Financial Risk* by Roger C. Gibson, who references the Talmud strategy. Both stress that a mixture of assets with different risks and rewards can give the best long-term return.

How to start?

Open an investment account at places like Charles Schwab, Vanguard, or Fidelity. Through these companies, you can invest in stocks, bonds, and real estate in the United States or abroad. Check to see which has the most advantageous services and lowest fees—lower fees mean more money for you, the investor.

How might I invest this money to start?

I suggest that you use the "couch potato" investment philosophy of Scott Burns while you are learning. You can Google this and read all about it. Essentially, this is a simple mixture of no-load mutual funds (no-load means no sales commissions or other fees). Choose to invest in a simple portfolio of one-third stocks, one-third bonds, and one-third real estate, realizing that a minimum dollar investment might be required.

How important is it to invest regularly?

In my opinion, this is crucial. If you have to decide each paycheck whether to invest or not, you are not likely to be successful. And money that you automatically invest is not missed. You adjust your spending to accommodate your take-home pay.

For example, if you invest 10 percent of your salary at 8 percent (less that the market has actually returned) for thirty-seven years, you will have twenty times your salary saved. If you invest 20 percent of your salary, you can accomplish this in about twenty-eight years. When you have twenty times your salary, you can withdraw your salary sum each year by using just 5 percent of that total to provide your annual salary without working! As Bob Brinker says, you have achieved critical mass at that point and no longer need to work for your money.

Once you have made your decision, the process is mainly mechanical with the need to regularly check in on your investments. If you dig in and learn about investments and their potential, you can be a very successful investor who is able to help your family and others all your life. Happy investing!

•

Eleven

Granddaddy's Summer Camp

One of the most enjoyable activities that Linda and I have been able to do with our nine grandchildren and their mothers is Granddaddy's Summer Camp at our fifty-acre river ranch in College Station, Texas. Our first camp was held in July 2006, and we have had it every year through this writing in 2018. We come together for a week of just having fun together. The camp started with eight children since the first was before our youngest grandchild, Chiara Shawver, was born in 2007, but has included all nine every year since then.

The idea came from my friend Dr. John Hoffmann who has a consulting engineering firm, Safety Engineering Laboratories, Inc., and farm in Michigan. When I told John about buying our place in College Station, he encouraged me to hold Granddaddy's Summer Camp at our place to get the kids out of Houston and Dallas, where they live and enjoy each other's company in the country. He and his wife had done this for many years and had enjoyed it tremendously. The name came from John even though my wife, Linda; our daughters, Jodi Malanga and Amy Shawver; and our daughter-in-law, Barbara Fowler, do most of the work! John and his wife continue it to the present, include grandkids and great-grandkids (now nineteen), and have combined it with a group charity project.

So we tried it; and on the first year, we went swimming, played games, went fishing in the Brazos River on our place, hit golf balls, rode horses, looked through the telescope to see Jupiter (no light pollution in the country), chased fireflies at night, shot off rockets, rode the zip line, played games, and just had a great time together. It was so much fun!

As the kids have grown, the activities have changed, with highlights every year, for example:

- 2006. Saw the stage production of *The Lion King* in Houston, went ice skating, horseback riding, swimming, saw the movie *Cars*, took golf cart rides, and had fun with the water hose sprinkler.
- 2007. Went horseback riding and swimming, visited the Blue Bell Creameries in Brenham, had lunch at the '50s diner at the Brenham Airport, shot off rockets, played in the playhouse, and had a piñata!
- 2008. Rode go-karts and horses, shot off rockets, played a laser tag game, had a talent show and painted T-shirts, went fishing and for golf cart rides, went to DoubleDave's Pizzaworks, Marble Slab Creamery, Martha's Bloomers, and had Coke floats!
- 2009. Rode go-karts and horses; went swimming; wore poodle skirts; went to Martha's Bloomers in Navasota and to Miramont Fun Day; had a talent show; witnessed the birth of the Blue Sword Company (Jack Malanga, proprietor); practiced archery; saw rockets; and played golf.
- 2010. Toured the George W. Bush Presidential Library at Texas A&M and Disaster City at the Fireman's Training Center; saw fireworks and rockets; went swimming, bowling, laser tagging, golfing, horseback riding, and shooting skeet at the shooting range.
- 2011. Went swimming and bowling; had pizza; played golf (ten golfers at Miramont) and bumper pool; went to the Blue Bell Creameries and Martha's Bloomers; played go-karts and golf carts; and went skeet shooting, catching fireflies, and stargazing; and ate s'mores.
- 2012. Had Nonna's party, went swimming and deer watching, went to Brenham Airport and to Martha's Bloomers, played nine golfers at Miramont, had a talent show, watched racing model cars, had teams competing in a scavenger hunt, saw

fireworks, went to a rifle shooting at the Brazos River, had Coke floats, and played in the newly remodeled barn and air hockey.
- 2013. Had Nonna's traditional opening party; went to Brenham Airport and Martha's Bloomers; went bowling, swimming, golfing, skeet shooting, rifle practicing; watched Big Dance and Talent Show!; played golf; had more fireworks and ice cream; went metal detecting and digging for fossils at the river; and went swimming and playing with the neighbor's dogs in the pool.
- 2014. Went swimming, partying, bowling, laser tagging; killed a copperhead in the garage; went to Washington-on-the-Brazos and Barrington, a working replica of Anson Jones's home (last president of the Republic of Texas) as he lived in the 1880s; played ten golfers at Miramont; went to Brenham Airport and joined the tour of the Offshore Drilling Exhibit at the Bush Library; had Rob's and Zack's birthday parties, and went shooting at the river.
- 2015. Went swimming, bowling, laser tagging; went to Martha's Bloomers, Miramont Day, DoubleDave's Pizzaworks, Marble Slab Creamery; and ate summer treats by the pool after golf. This camp was abbreviated in favor of our fiftieth wedding anniversary when we took all our grandkids and their parents to Banff, Canada, for a fun time.
- 2016. Had Nonna's party, learned trigonometry to measure tree heights, joined a walking tour by Jeff Ledlow (licensed arborist) to identify all sixteen types of trees at the River Ranch, played seven golfers at Miramont, went to Martha's Bloomers, Granddaddy fell into the swimming pool fully clothed, kids worked out at the Student Rec Center at A&M, Robert surprised Zack to celebrate his fifteenth birthday, did Nonna's art project, kids made Granddaddy a special book for his seventieth birthday, and celebrated Barb's birthday at the Republic Steakhouse.
- 2017. Ate pizza; went swimming, laser tagging, bowling; had thumb wars; toured the Royalty Pecan Farms and store at Caldwell; had many more workouts at Student Rec Center; the girls did Nick's curls; went dancing to George Strait; drank

Coke floats; went to Martha's Bloomers; celebrated Zack's birthday; played golf at Miramont; and had lunch by the pool.
- 2018. Went swimming, bowling, laser tagging, golfing; went to Martha's Bloomers, to a seminar on how to write a book by Pam Wilkinson, and a seminar and roundtable on grandchildren's advice for raising children; had more workouts at Student Rec Center; and played at the River Ranch.

From this, you can see that we have continued the camp each year so we have had thirteen in total. As the children grew older, activities changed to suit what they like to do, but the time together is the same. We always try to have some educational activity, and since many of the campers are so talented, we usually have a talent show. This year (2018), we had a special activity when Pam Wilkinson, my collaborator on this book, came; and we had a facilitated discussion about the grandchildren's thoughts regarding what is important in raising children. The section of this book "Grandchildren's Advice for Raising Kids" is a recap of their comments from that session.

All the grandkids really want to continue this annual event even though everyone recognizes the difficulties as they grow up and begin their careers and start their own families. This year, the oldest grandson camper was Jack Malanga, age twenty-one. We were lucky he was in summer school at Texas A&M in College Station and could make most of the activities. I would urge families to try something similar to enable children to build relationships and memories with their cousins—and enjoy those memories for years to come!

•

TWELVE

Grandchildren's Advice for Raising Kids

June 20, 2018

Parents and grandparents always have concerns about their offspring. One of mine is the influence of today's affluent society, especially compared with my own growing-up times. I decided to find out what our grandchildren think, and here are their thoughts.

The question posed was, What are the challenges of raising children in an affluent society? This was put to all the grandchildren—and one great-nephew—in a roundtable discussion at Granddaddy's Summer Camp 2018. Their ages ranged from eleven to twenty-one, six boys, four girls.* They zeroed in on four main topics, and it's interesting to see how the conversation piggybacked and circled around, tying it all together:

- Need for a moral compass
- Awareness of interpersonal relationships
- Developing a strong work ethic
- Developing independence

Everyone agreed that it is the parents' responsibility to give kids a coherent set of moral principles of what is right and what is wrong, and they proposed specific ideas. For example, when parents establish rules, they can't be arbitrary. It's not fair to say to kids, "Do this because I said so." The parents must give the kids the reason behind the rules so that the kids will learn to think for themselves.

The group thought that most things are clear from the moral compass, but some things are gray. In that case, kids need to be taught to seek advice and wisdom, maybe from a trusted teacher or other adult, if not your parents. Part of the moral compass includes finding religious purpose in your daily life because as somebody said, "Living just for yourself isn't going to be happy or fulfilling."

The group also was clear in thinking that the most important personal skill to develop is empathy. How can you have friends or develop leadership skills without empathy? Someone suggested that having experience with and exposure to animals is one way to develop empathy.

They expressed the belief that respect for others is very important as well. How can people respect you if you don't respect them? Kids should be taught to follow God's principle to "love everyone as yourself." And always be kind to everyone. Since all good relationships are based on mutual trust, maintaining that trust is basic to keeping the relationship intact.

The group then seized on the need to raise children with a strong work ethic. They believe hard work is the key to success and happiness. How about getting them to do homework instead of playing video games? They understood that parents must set and help kids develop expectations. For example, parents should teach kids, "You can get this or achieve that, but you have to be willing to work for it." Another somebody said that kids need to learn they can't have everything and realize how fortunate they truly are.

They suggested that doing volunteer work is a very good way for kids to understand their own personal circumstances. They suggested that many times, homeless people suffer depression and mental problems that keep them from becoming successful adults, and understanding that through direct experience helps to develop empathy.

Next, in order to develop independence, kids should be allowed to form their own opinions as much as possible, within the boundaries of their earlier discussion on moral guidance. Parents must help kids to learn to trust their own values. Picking friends, and later spouses, needs to be mainly based on character because someone with poor character will not make a good friend or spouse. In the end, functioning adults must be able to think for themselves.

Grandchildren's Advice for Raising Kids

The group also talked about the importance of learning resilience in life and how to get back up when life knocks you down. Everyone should get their approval from themselves and God and not from others. You can't really learn this from a book, but life experiences where kids have to develop resilience are very important. Parents can help by suggesting and supporting challenging projects. Running a small business like a lemonade stand, lawn mowing, or pet sitting is great experience; and at some point, young people need experience working for someone besides a parent. Parents should encourage their kids to take chances with their life and grow!

Another big part of independence is becoming financially independent. For that to happen, young people should be educated in developing financial skills. Someone remembered that our family ran a family investment club for a number of years as Jodi and John, Rob and Barb, and Amy and Robert started their adult lives. The goal of all parents and young people is to have the young folks become financially independent.

Having sat in on this discussion, I think that the next generation is in very good hands! I remember Linda and I felt that raising children was pretty much equal parts of love and discipline. Too much love and not enough discipline, and the children have trouble with independence. Too much discipline and not enough love leads to children without sufficient self-confidence. Starvation of either love or discipline leads to all sorts of adult problems.

In many ways, a family is like a company with its distinct culture. Probably the most important thing to get right is a family culture that is loving and supportive and has as its primary goal: the proper raising of the next generation.

*Participating grandchildren were as follows: Jack Malanga, age twenty-one; Nick Malanga, age eighteen; Annaliese Fower, age seventeen; Zack Shawver, age seventeen; Olivia Fowler, age fifteen; Daniel Shawver, age fifteen; Samantha Fowler, age thirteen; Alex Malanga, age twelve; Chiara Shawver, age eleven; and participating great-nephew, Micah Tardy, age twenty.

•

Fowler Family Portrait, December 2018.

TIMELINE

Stress Engineering Services Inc.

- 1972. Company founded by Joe Fowler, Ray Latham, and Harry Sweet.
  Work was certified stress reports for nuclear power plants and support of deep, high-pressure gas wells.
- 1974. Tom Asbill, Allen Fox, and Bob Wink joined the firm.
- 1975. Ron Young and Teri Shackelford joined the firm. Ron began work on DERP (frequency domain riser program).
  Start of floating systems practice.
- 1976. Jack Miller joined the firm.
- 1977. Richard Boswell joined the firm.
- 1978. Randy Long joined the firm.
- 1980. Chuck Miller joined the firm.
  Mobil project led to establishment of the first test lab.
- 1981. John Chappell joined the firm.
- 1984. Upheaval in the firm.
- 1985. Jim Albert joined the firm.
  Start of M&C practice.
- 1986. Firm moved to our present building.
- 1987. Secured Conoco Joliet project (rigs and risers).
  Chris Matice started with the firm (CFD practice origins).
- 1988. Started work for Procter & Gamble.
  Jack Miller returned.
- 1990. David Tekamp joined the firm and opened the Cincinnati office.

Stress Engineering Services Inc.

- 1991. Clint Haynes and Terry Lechinger joined the firm.
    Four-million-pound load frame installed.
- 1992. Paul Kovach joined the firm and began our materials practice.
- 1995. Shell Auger and outside load frames.
- 1996. Opened the New Orleans office; Greg Garic and Glen Aucoin joined the firm.
- 1997. Claudio Allevato started the AE practice at Stress Engineering Services Inc.
- 1999. Bought Mohr Engineering from Oil States Industries.
- 2000. September 1, 2000, was the death of Wayne Clampett.
    Bought assets of ERA Inc. from ERA Ltd.
    Bobby Wright joined the firm.
    Opened the Chicago office.
    Dave Garrett joined the firm. Had the RAMS development.
- 2002. Started the Baton Rouge office.
- 2003. Opened Mohr Building.
    Stress subsea started (Kerry Kirkland).
- 2004. Bought subsea building.
- 2005. Completed new Houston lab building.
    Completed six-million-pound frame.
    ESOP started.
- 2007. Formal strategic planning process started.
    Bought ninety-four acres in Waller, Texas, for expansion.
    Started on new green office building in Houston.
    Bought 8.5 acres on I-71 in Mason, Ohio, for expansion.
- 2008. Bought 8505 Westland for M&C and AE.
- 2009. Completed Houston LEED-certified building.
    Started Cincinnati creep lab.
    Bought property in Metairie, Louisiana, to expand facility.
- 2010. Opened Waller lab and H_2S testing facility.
    Completed NOV building at Waller.
    Opened Cincinnati creep lab.

- 2011. Purchased Zeus Engineering in Calgary, Canada.
    Robert Thom joined the firm.
    Completed culture definition project.
    Started third Waller building and new Cincinnati building.
    New corporate QMS director, Earl Hudspeth, starts.
    New Orleans building finished.
    Loss of Tom Asbill and retirement of Bob Wink—both big losses.
- 2012. Fortieth anniversary celebration.
    Built building three in Waller.
    Finished Cincinnati building.
    Elastomer testing/analysis practice.
- 2013. Building four at Waller started (fifty thousand square feet).
    Strategic planning effort.
    Richard Boswell and Teri Shackelford formally retired.
- 2015 Started Stress Engineering & Construction.
    David Masterson joined the firm.
    Started full-scale test lab in Singapore.
    Jack Miller succeeded Joe Fowler as president.

•

RESOURCES

Some material in this book has appeared in other formats, lectures, or presentations by Joe R. Fowler. "What's in a Name?" from chapter 5 was written after his tenure as president of Stress Engineering Services Inc. and appears on the company website.

•

Brinker, Bob. *Bob Brinker's Marketview*. Retrieved January 12, 2019. www.bobbrinker.com.

Confucius quotation. Retrieved January 10, 2019. www.brainyquote.com/quotes/confucius_131984.

Culture eats strategy quotation. Retrieved May 23, 2018. www.forbes.com.

Davy, Humphry. Inventor of the miner's safety lamp. Retrieved January 8, 2019. www.famousscientists.org

Gensler, Arthur and Michael Lindenmayer. 2015. *Art's Principles*. Wilson Lafferty.

Harmon, Claude, Jr. and Steve Eubanks. 2006. *The Pro: Lessons about Golf and Life from My Father, Claude Harmon, Sr.* Crown Publishing Group, Random House.

Hoffmann, J. M., D. J. Hoffmann, E. C. Kroll, J. J. Kroll, L. M. Logan, and J. R. Fowler. 2003. "Effectiveness of Gas Fired Water Heater Elevation in the Reduction of Ignition Vapors from Flammable Liquid Spills." *Fire Technology*, 39.

John Wesley quotation. Retrieved February 25, 2018. www.forbes.com.

McFerrin, Artie. 2014. *The Executioner: Implementing Intangible, Elusive Success Principles*. Archway Publishing.

Moore's Law. Retrieved January 12, 2019. www.en.wikopedia.org.

Resources

National Center for Employee Ownership. Retrieved June 9, 2018. www.nceo.org.

Proverbs 15:22. Retrieved May 23, 2018. www.biblegateway.com.

Proverbs 22:29. Retrieved May 23, 2018. www.biblegateway.com.

Stewardship definition. Retrieved February 26, 2018. www.merriam-webster.com.

Stress Engineering Services, Inc. www.stress.com

Steinmetz, Lawrence W. 2005. "The Right Stuff on Time." In *How to Sell at Prices Higher than Your Competitors*. Wiley.

"The Talmud Strategy." Retrieved May 23, 2018. www.financial-planning.com/news/the-talmud-strategy.

•

ABOUT THE AUTHOR

Joe R. Fowler

Joe R. Fowler was raised in Wichita Falls, Texas; graduated from Wichita Falls High School; and received his BS with honors, MS, and PhD degrees in mechanical engineering from Texas A&M University. He worked two years for Texaco in drilling research and then cofounded Stress Engineering Services Inc. (SES) in 1972. He became president in 1984.

During his thirty-one years as president, SES compounded sales at 15.5 percent annually and profited at 19.7 percent annually. The company grew to become a 430-person engineering consulting firm based in Houston and Waller with additional offices in Cincinnati, New Orleans, Calgary, and Singapore. SES is a world leader in floating systems design, fitness-for-service evaluations, and EPC services to the process industries, consumer-product mechanical design, measurement and control systems, and third-party testing of full-scale systems and equipment.

In 2010, SES was named the No. 1 Best Place to Work in Texas and the No. 2 Best Place to Work in Ohio. In 2011–2014, the company was cited on the *Houston Chronicle* "List of the Best Places to Work in Houston" and was named the No. 3 Best Place to Work in Ohio and one of the best places to work in New Orleans. In 2018, Stress celebrated its forty-sixth year in business and has twice been named in the Aggie 100.

Stress is 100 percent an employee-owned company, and every full-time employee has a stake in the company after a year's service.

Turnover rate has been below 4 percent for many years. One reason is the 360-degree peer evaluations each year where cooperation is measured and rewarded. More than eight hundred clients come to Stress each year for their most difficult problems. The technical staff (two-thirds with advanced degrees in engineering) loves the challenge.

Dr. Fowler has authored twenty-eight technical publications and five patents. In 2015, he received an American Society of Civil Engineers Hall of Fame Award for pioneering work in offshore pipelines. In 2014, he was inducted into the Offshore Energy Center Technology Hall of Fame for his work on marine risers used in offshore drilling. He is a registered professional engineer in Texas. He is a fellow of the American Society of Mechanical Engineers (ASME), and in 2000, he received the Outstanding Alumni Honor Award from the Dwight Look College of Engineering at Texas A&M University. He received the Rhodes Oil Drop Industry Leader Award in 2003 and the Titanium Crawfish Award for oil industry achievements from ASME and the University of Houston in 2004. In 2000–2001, he served as president of ABET, which accredits all engineering, technology, applied science, and computer science programs in the USA.

Currently, he serves as chair of the advisory council of the Dwight Look College of Engineering at Texas A&M University. He is immediate past chair of the Board of Directors of the Offshore Technology Conference and on the Board of Directors of the Pearl Fincher Museum and the Endowment Board of Northwest Assistance Ministries. In 2012, he was named Ernst & Young Entrepreneur of the Year in the business services category for the Gulf Coast region of the United States. In 2017, he was elected to serve on the Board of Governors of ASME.

He and his wife, Linda, enjoy their three children along with their spouses and nine grandchildren. In 2015, they celebrated their fiftieth wedding anniversary. They help many charities supporting higher education for deserving youth and local Houston charities for citizens in need and the arts.

•

Printed in the United States
By Bookmasters